Lake District
day BY day™

1st Edition

by Louise McGrath

WILEY

A John Wiley and Sons, Ltd, Publication

Contents

9up.2
FROMMERS

UK Publisher: Sally Smith
Production Manager: Daniel Mersey
Commissioning Editor: Mark Henshall
Development Editor: Lindsay Hunt
Project Editor: Hannah Clement
Photo Research: David Cottingham
Cartography: Jeremy Norton

British Library Cataloguing in Publication Data
A catalogue record for this book is available from the British Library

ISBN: 978-0-470-71555-0

Typeset by Wiley Indianapolis Composition Services
Printed and bound in China by RR Donnelley

5 4 3 2 1

A Note from the Editorial Director

Organizing your time. That's what this guide is all about.

Other guides give you long lists of things to see and do and then expect you to fit the pieces together. The Day by Day guides are different. These guides tell you the best of everything, and then they show you how to see it *in the smartest, most time-efficient way*. Our authors have designed detailed itineraries organized by time, neighborhood, or special interest. And each tour comes with a bulleted map that takes you from stop to stop.

Hoping to reach the summit of Scafell Pike, England's highest peak, relax on a lake cruise on Windermere or sit to read some poetry in Wordsworth's summerhouse at Rydal Mount? Planning to walk through Beatrix Potter's garden at Hill Top Farm or relax in a pub by a roaring fire, sampling seasonal Cumbrian cuisine and local ales? Whatever your interest or schedule, the Day by Days give you the smartest routes to follow. Not only do we take you to the top attractions, hotels, and restaurants, but we also help you access those special moments that locals get to experience—those "finds" that turn tourists into travelers.

The Day by Days are also your top choice if you're looking for one complete guide for all your travel needs. The best hotels and restaurants for every budget, the greatest shopping values, the wildest nightlife—it's all here.

Why should you trust our judgment? Because our authors personally visit each place they write about. They're an independent lot who say what they think and would never include places they wouldn't recommend to their best friends. They're also open to suggestions from readers. If you'd like to contact them, please send your comments our way at feedback@frommers.com, and we'll pass them on.

Enjoy your Day by Day guide—the most helpful travel companion you can buy. And have the trip of a lifetime.

Warm regards,

Kelly Regan

Kelly Regan, Editorial Director
Frommer's Travel Guides

About the Author

Louise McGrath, a freelance writer and editor, has lived in England, the USA, Colombia, Spain and now Northern Ireland. She's written/updated several guidebooks to Portugal and Ireland as well as dozens of guides worldwide for Whatsonwhen.

Acknowledgments

A big thank you to Cumbria Tourism for facilitating and sponsoring my exploration of the Lake District, especially to Julie Darroch, whose contacts and enthusiasm smoothed my path. Thanks also to Frommer's Commissioning Editor Mark Henshall for his support and patience, and to my brother, Mike, based in the Lake District, for his spare room and local knowledge as well as his physiotherapy skills, which got me back on my feet following a back injury. I'm also ever grateful to my husband, Sean, for accompanying me across the fells and for taking numerous photographs.

An Additional Note

Please be advised that travel information is subject to change at any time—and this is especially true of prices. We therefore suggest that you write or call ahead for confirmation when making your travel plans. The authors, editors, and publisher cannot be held responsible for the experiences of readers while traveling. Your safety is important to us, however, so we encourage you to stay alert and be aware of your surroundings.

Star Ratings, Icons & Abbreviations

Every hotel, restaurant, and attraction listing in this guide has been ranked for quality, value, service, amenities, and special features using a **star-rating** system. Hotels, restaurants, attractions, shopping, and nightlife are rated on a scale of zero stars (recommended) to three stars (exceptional). In addition to the star-rating system, we also use a **kids** icon to point out the best bets for families. Within each tour, we recommend cafes, bars, or restaurants where you can take a break. Each of these stops appears in a shaded box marked with a coffee-cup-shaped bullet 🍵.

The following **abbreviations** are used for credit cards:

AE	American Express	DISC	Discover	V	Visa
DC	Diners Club	MC	MasterCard		

Travel Resources at Frommers.com

Now that you have this guidebook to help you plan a great trip, visit our website at **www.frommers.com** for additional travel information on more than 4,000 destinations. We update features regularly to give you instant access to the most current trip-planning information available. At Frommers.com, you'll find scoops on the best airfares, lodging rates, and car rental bargains. You can even book your travel online through our reliable travel booking partners. Other popular features include:

A Note on Prices

In the "Take a Break" and "Best Bets" sections of this book, we have used a system of dollar signs to show a range of costs for 1 night in a hotel (the price of a double-occupancy room) or the cost of an entree (main course) at a restaurant. Use the following table to decipher the dollar signs:

Cost	Hotels	Restaurants
$	under $100	under $10
$$	$100–$200	$10–$20
$$$	$200–$300	$20–$30
$$$$	$300–$400	$30–$40
$$$$$	over $400	over $40

How to Contact Us

In researching this book, we discovered many wonderful places—hotels, restaurants, shops, and more. We're sure you'll find others. Please tell us about them, so we can share the information with your fellow travelers in upcoming editions. If you were disappointed with a recommendation, we'd love to know that, too. Please write to:

Frommer's Lake District Day by Day, 1st Edition
Wiley Publishing, Inc. • 111 River St. • Hoboken, NJ 07030-5774

20 Favourite
Moments

20 Favourite **Moments**

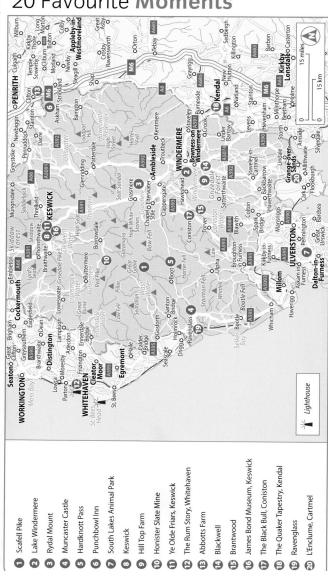

✴ *Lighthouse*

1 Scafell Pike
2 Lake Windermere
3 Rydal Mount
4 Muncaster Castle
5 Hardknott Pass
6 Punchbowl Inn
7 South Lakes Animal Park
8 Keswick
9 Hill Top Farm
10 Honister Slate Mine
11 Ye Olde Friars, Keswick
12 The Rum Story, Whitehaven
13 Abbotts Farm
14 Blackwell
15 Brantwood
16 James Bond Museum, Keswick
17 The Black Bull, Coniston
18 The Quaker Tapestry, Kendal
19 Ravenglass
20 L'Enclume, Cartmel

Visitors have been drawn to the Lake District for generations, hoping to experience the drama of its highest fells and deepest lakes, whether it is draped in spring daffodils or bathed in autumn hues. The striking scenery is enhanced by pretty Lakeland villages, seasonal Cumbrian menus and literary heroes like Potter, Wordsworth and Ruskin, making it an attractive destination throughout the year. Below are 20 of my favourite Lake District experiences.

1 Reaching the summit of Scafell Pike, England's highest peak. The first part of the ascent is the most difficult, with what seems like an endless uphill climb alongside a stream. But you're rewarded at every turn by the views of Wastwater below, and at the top the sense of achievement makes the effort all worthwhile. *See p 151.*

2 Relaxing on a lake cruise on Windermere. As the boat glides through the water, you're blessed with far-reaching views of the glistening water, framed by green hills and the occasional country mansion. *See p 12.*

3 Sitting in the Poet's summerhouse at Rydal Mount. You can just imagine William Wordsworth practising his poetry while strolling along the terrace here, or taking inspiration as he sat taking in the view beyond the trees to Rydal Water and Dora's Field. *See p 36.*

4 Feeling a chill in the Tapestry Room at Muncaster Castle. Stay here all night on a ghost-hunting trip—if you dare. *For more information, see p 42.*

Taking in the view from the top of Scafell Pike.

Wordsworth's summerhouse at Rydal Mount.

5 Zigzagging round hairpin beds across Hardknott Pass. As you drive along this winding road, the terrain becomes rocky and its valleys remote, but you're rewarded with a spectacular panorama. If you time it well, the sunset creates a special glow across the landscape, enhancing the colours of each season. *See p 87*.

6 Sitting by a roaring fire in the Punchbowl Inn and Restaurant. On New Year's Day the landlord at this pub in Askham roasts a hog on a spit outside the bar. During my visit the snow lay thick on the ground and there was a power cut, but we sat in candlelight around a roaring fire and munched on pork and apple sandwiches. Idyllic. *See p 77*.

7 Meeting the wildlife at South Lakes Animal Park. Kids love the comical giraffes here, and the monkeys with their fringes brushed diagonally across their foreheads like teenagers. *See p 93*.

8 Following the bands around Keswick's pubs. Each year, Keswick hosts a jazz festival with renowned British, American and European musicians. Both trad and mainstream bands perform in various locations around the town. *See p 172*.

9 Walking through Beatrix Potter's garden at Hill Top Farm. Visits to the house are by timed tickets, so explore the garden while you wait. The cottage garden is a treat in summer. *See p 119*.

10 Facing your fears on the via ferrata at Honister Slate Mine. This system of cables and footholds means you can traverse a rock face with no previous climbing experience. If your kids are big enough, they can try it too, or opt for a mine tour deep inside the mountain. *See p 58*.

11 Spoilt for choice at Ye Olde Friars sweet shop in Keswick. This shop is a candy fantasyland with sweets piled high in all colours, shapes and sizes. *See p 53.*

12 **Discovering Whitehaven's maritime past at The Rum Story.** This entertaining museum is full of sound effects and life-sized models depicting the rum trade—and the heartbreaking slave trade that came with it. *See p 144.*

13 **Eating ice cream at Abbott's Farm.** A perfect way to entertain the kids with indoor and outdoor play areas, a chance to meet the cows and their calves and fresh ice cream made on the premises. *See p 60.*

14 **Visiting Blackwell, an Arts and Crafts gem near Windermere.** It's hard to believe that this beautiful house with its exuberant decorative details was rescued from almost total dilapidation. Today it shows off the fine craftsmanship of the wood-panelled hall and the white drawing room. *See p 45.*

15 **Taking tea at Brantwood.** The best way to get to John Ruskin's

Ravenglass & Eskdale Railway.

house is to take a ride on the steam yacht *Gondola* from Coniston. A refreshment stop at the café

Beatrix Potter's garden at Hill Top Farm.

Facing my fears at Honister Slate Mine.

overlooking Coniston Water completes a satisfying trip. *See p 44.*

⑯ Seeing the Aston Martin DB5 from Goldeneye. The James Bond Museum in Keswick has an astounding collection of vehicles featured in Bond films, including Dr No and Casino Royale. *See p 130.*

⑰ Sipping the ales at the Black Bull in Coniston. The real ales brewed at the back of the pub could give more famous brands a run for their money. It's a fine example of several micro-breweries dotted throughout the Lake District. *See p 113.*

⑱ Admiring the needlework at the Quaker Tapestry. This award-winning museum is a tribute to the dedication and commitment of the volunteers that have created these tapestries; and to the history of the philanthropic Quaker movement. *See p 124.*

⑲ Riding the steam train from Ravenglass to Eskdale. It's a short journey, but a fun way to travel up the valley, with picturesque stops on the way. Just beyond the end of the line is Hardknott Roman Fort. *See p 87 and p 177.*

⑳ Indulging your taste buds at L'Enclume. This Michelin-starred restaurant in Cartmel promises a real treat. The emphasis is on subtle flavours, each mouth-watering dish immaculately and artistically presented with a dash of sauce or a carefully placed flower. *See p 94.* ●

1 Strategies for Seeing the Region

Strategies for Seeing the Region

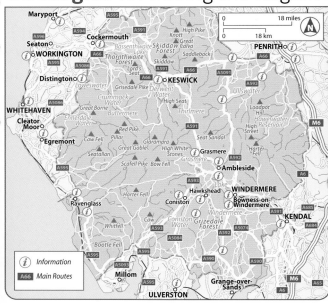

The Lake District National Park measures just 30 miles across but within this boundary lie locations that are remote and almost inaccessible. So planning your days is as important as choosing your base, with activities and attractions to suit outdoor enthusiasts, families and couples on a romantic getaway. The pointers below are here to help you make the most of your trip.

Rule #1. Weigh up the pros and cons of taking or hiring a car

It doesn't really need to be spelt out that a car is useful for getting to places off the beaten track. After all, it gives you the freedom to just get up and go; especially useful with a family in tow. And what better place to take your car than the country roads of the Lake District? Except when you're stuck in a queue or searching for a car parking space, and it feels like everyone else has had exactly the same idea. During peak season, traffic queues build up throughout the Lake District's most popular areas, particularly between Bowness, Ambleside and Grasmere. This has a knock-on effect on parking. Seriously, you might have to hunt down a parking space in peak season, particularly in smaller villages where space is at a premium. Parking costs add up, so allow for that. Even in the countryside, many parking places are operated by the National Trust or Lake District National Park and will charge a fee (National Trust members can usually park free of charge. See box below.

Rule #2. Check your car
Traffic generally flows fairly swiftly along the 'A' roads around the edge of the Lake District and there are several towns en route where you can stop for fuel or refreshments. But this isn't so along some of the mountain passes (Hardknott and Wrynose, Kirkstone or Honister), where the roads are steep, winding and remote. Make sure your tyres are in good condition and that you have plenty of fuel and oil before you set off on these roads.

Rule #3. Consider travelling by bus or train
Even if you have travelled to the Lake District by car, you don't need to use it the entire time you're there. A convenient bus network links the most popular towns (p 176). You can buy day or weekly tickets and hop on and off the buses without having to worry about parking. There are also mainline train services to the South Lakes, Cumbrian coast, West Lakes and Windermere (Savvy Traveler p 169), as well as steam train trips between Lakeside and Haverthwaite (p 56), and Ravenglass and Eskdale (p 87).

Rule #4. Consider where you are going to stay
I've suggested a range of accommodation options in this guide to suit different tastes. You'll find them listed at the end of each town guide and each regional guide. These include B&Bs in villages, guest houses in the country, self-catering apartments in town and cottages in the hills. There are also some luxury lakeside hotels and camping and caravanning sites by the sea, lakes and in forest parks, some with chalets and even yurts (Mongolian nomadic dwellings made from wooden frames covered in felt).

Rule #5. Think about the children
Campsites tend to be more family-orientated; some hotels cater well for children but check in advance to see what facilities are provided on-site or

Lake District Floods

In November 2009, Cumbria experienced the most severe flooding in its history. The Lake District was engulfed with raging floods following the heaviest rainfall ever recorded in Britain. Thousands were affected by the devastation, with roads and bridges closed and flood-hit communities in Cumbria cut off as the county's infrastructure was severely damaged. As well as communities, homes and businesses, important historical points of interest such as Wordsworth House in Cockermouth were also affected. Visitors to the Lake District should be aware that communities and organisations such as the National Trust have pulled together to work hard in helping each other, putting walls up, repairing paths, rebuilding their environment and connecting this beautiful landscape back to the rest of the world. This is a close-knit community and we urge you to help this wonderful region as you travel through it and be sympathetic to its people who are slowly rebuilding their lives.

nearby. See the Lake District with Kids section (p 54) and the Outdoors chapter (p 147) for attractions and activities suitable for children.

Rule #6. Time your visit right

Plan your trip according to your interests. Garden enthusiasts might want to come in the spring for the carpets of daffodils and bluebells or in autumn to see the swathes of gold and brown in the trees. Some houses close in the winter so check ahead. Find out whether popular events and festivals coincide with your visit, whether or not you plan to attend. Hotels and campsites also get booked up quickly during public and school holidays, so take that into account.

Rule #7. Plan your fell walking and cycling carefully

Inevitably, parts of the Lake District are remote; it is easy to misjudge a route direction, length and conditions without proper planning and foresight. If in any doubt, take a guided walk or opt for something shorter. Buy a good map (and a compass or even a GPS) and plan your route in advance. Pack a small rucksack or day bag with plenty of water, energy bars and suitable clothing, as well as a small first-aid kit. Don't underestimate how rapidly temperatures can drop, even if it is hot at your starting point. Take layers of clothing (a base layer, a warm baselayer, a hat and a windproof/waterproof outer layer) that you can peel off or add if necessary. Make sure your footwear is supportive and comfortable enough for the length of walk you're doing. Don't go out on long walks wearing boots that you haven't worn in or you might regret it after a couple of hours. And finally, check the weather conditions before you set off.

Rule #8. Travel with your mobile phone

Yes, it's a good idea to take your mobile phone and/or GPS (global positioning system) system whether walking, cycling or travelling by car. If you're stuck in the mountains, dial 999 and ask for Mountain Rescue. But be aware that you cannot always guarantee that you will have a signal. Make sure you always tell someone where you are going and what time to expect you back. If you follow other advice listed here, you will minimize any unforeseen problems. ●

Lake District Conservation

The huge numbers of people visiting the Lake District have a serious impact on its landscape and wildlife. The National Trust and the Lake District National Park (p 156), along with charitable organizations like The Friends of the Lake District (FLD) and The British Trust for Conservation Volunteers (BTCV) work with the tourist industry to protect the Lakes. But as visitors, we also have a responsibility to leave the countryside and wildlife as we find it, to minimize our impact on delicate ecosystems by not picking flowers, damaging paths, woodlands and nests, closing all gates after us, and by taking all our belongings and leftovers with us when we leave.

2 The Best Full-Day Tours

Lake District in a **Long Weekend**

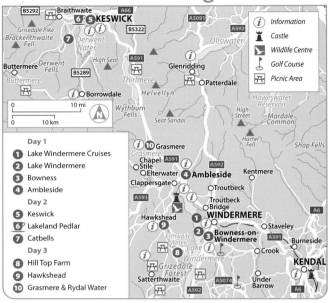

i	Information
🏰	Castle
📷	Wildlife Centre
🚩	Golf Course
🏕	Picnic Area

Day 1
1. Lake Windermere Cruises
2. Lake Windermere
3. Bowness
4. Ambleside

Day 2
5. Keswick
6. Lakeland Pedlar
7. Catbells

Day 3
8. Hill Top Farm
9. Hawkshead
10. Grasmere & Rydal Water

You can pack a lot into a weekend in the Lake District, but if you have limited time, what matters is to pick the right base. Staying somewhere near Windermere or Grasmere gives you swift access to a variety of attractions and scenery. My suggestions below include boat trips, visits to Bowness-on-Windermere, Ambleside, Hawkshead and Grasmere, and a hill walk up Catbells.

Day One

1 ★★★ Lake Windermere Cruises. It's easy to spend a whole day around **Windermere**, starting with a leisurely boat trip. Trips from **Bowness** are slightly shorter and less time-consuming than those from Ambleside, but just as scenic. Choose from cruise-and-attraction tickets, 24- or 48-hour hop-on, hop-off tickets, or cruises around the islands. *Bowness Pier.* ☎ *015394 43360. www.windermere-lakecruises. co.uk, Tickets 24-hour Freedom of the Lake £11.60 adults; £5.80 children;* *£31.50 family. Timetable summer approx 9.15am–6.45pm; winter 10am–4.15pm (check timetable for individual routes). Bus 555.*

2 ★★★ Lake Windermere. The best things to do around Windermere are to take a boat to Lakeside, visit the **Lakes Aquarium** (see p 56, **2**), enjoy a steam-train ride on the **Lakeside & Haverthwaite Railway** (see p 56, **3**) and take a ferry across to **Fell Foot Park** for a picnic. You can hire bicycles in Lakeside from Country Lanes (see p 157),

Enjoy a leisurely cruise on Windermere.

then head through **Grizedale Forest** on a network of cycle paths (p 155). Alternatively, enjoy some of the many lakeshore walks: e.g. from Lakeside through fields and woodland, to Beatrix Potter's **Hill Top Farm** (see p 31, ❸), or from Bowness/Ferry House and **Ambleside Roman Fort** (see p 99, ❼).

❸ ★ **Bowness.** The town of Windermere leads downhill past souvenir shops, boutiques and galleries and merges into Bowness, which spreads along the banks of Windermere lake. Tourists wait for boats at Bowness Pier, relax with ice creams on the wide grass verge, feed the swans and admire the views. Enjoy fish n' chips by the pier or a more substantial meal at one of the nearby grand hotels. My favourite attraction in Bowness is the **World of Beatrix Potter** (p 30, ❶), ideal for young children. *Bus 555 from Keswick, Grasmere, Ambleside and Kendal. For a full tour of Bowness see p 102.*

❹ ★ **Ambleside. Horse-drawn carriages** or taxis will take you from the pier to the town centre if you don't fancy walking. Ambleside is

renowned for its **outdoor clothing** and equipment shops, and is well-stocked with **cafes and pubs** such as the Apple Pie and the Royal Oak. If you're feeling energetic, walk up to the spectacular **Stock Ghyll Force** waterfall. Stop to take some snaps of 17th-century Bridge House or discover something about Lakeland personalities at the **Armitt Museum**. *Bus 555 from Keswick, Grasmere, Bowness and Kendal. For a full tour of Ambleside see p 96.*

Day Two

❺ ★ **Keswick.** Keswick's position near several well-known fells (the local word for hills or mountains) makes it popular with walkers. It is set at the north end of Derwentwater; a boat ride is one of the most popular activities. Keswick has several attractions, including the **Cumberland Pencil Museum, Keswick Museum & Art Gallery, Cars of the Stars** and the **James Bond Museum**. Check the schedule of the **Theatre by the Lake** for theatre, dance and music performances. *Bus 555 from Grasmere, Ambleside, Bowness and Kendal. For a full tour of Keswick, see p 128.*

There are clear tracks to the top of Catbells.

Take a Break

6 Lakeland Pedlar. I am not a vegetarian but I return again and again to this wholefood café for its substantial healthy options. Eat in or take away a sandwich or snack for your afternoon walk. There's a bicycle shop upstairs. *Bell Close.* ☎ *017687 74492. www.lakeland pedlar.co.uk. Open daily 9am–5pm. Mains from £6.95.*

7 ★ Catbells. This is a good fell walk for youngsters. Whatever your fitness level, it's a rewarding climb for the spectacular views across Derwentwater towards Skiddaw and the eastern crags near Crummock Water. Most people approach Catbells by taking the ferry across to **Hawes End** and returning from **Low Brandlehow**. *See p 150, Chapter 6 for more details of the walk and various routes.*

Day Three
8 ★ Hill Top Farm. Start the day at Beatrix Potter's former home of Hill Top (p 31, **3**), a 17th-century

cottage in Near Sawrey. As you walk up to the cottage from the car park, look out for one of her characters, **Mr McGregor**, well a life-size model, sitting outside Buckle Yeat Guest House, next to the Tower Bank Arms pub. *Near Sawrey.* ☎ *015394 36269.*

Potter character Mr McGregor can often be seen sitting outside Buckle Yeat B&B in Near Sawrey.

Hawkshead is one of the Lake District's prettiest villages.

www.nationaltrust.org.uk. *Admission £5.80 adults; £2.90 children; £14.50 family. Opening times house mid-Mar–Oct Mon–Thur, Sat and Sun 10.30am–4.30pm, shop/garden Feb and Nov–Dec daily 10.30am–4.30pm, 1st two weeks Mar Sat and Sun 10am–4pm, mid-Mar–Oct daily 10am–4pm. Transport: ferry from Bowness to Ferry House and walk to Near Sawrey* 🕐 *40 min.*

9 ★ **Hawkshead.** From Near Sawrey it's just a ten-minute drive (or 40-minute walk) to the pretty village of **Hawkshead**, where you'll find **Hawkshead Grammar School**, once attended by Wordsworth (see p 119, **3**) and the **Beatrix Potter Gallery** (see p 120, **6**). *Bus 505. For a full tour of Hawkshead see p 118.*

10 ★ **Grasmere & Rydal Water.** Tourists, walkers, artists and literary fans all converge on Grasmere in peak season. It is a very picturesque village, which is why Wordsworth spent his most creative years living at **Dove Cottage**. Grasmere is also home to the **Wordsworth family graves** and Sarah Nelson's famous **Grasmere Gingerbread Shop**. Rydal Water lies just a short distance down the road; if you have time, visit **Rydal Mount and Gardens,** Wordsworth's last home (p 36, **3**). *Bus 599. For a full tour of Grasmere see p 114.*

Grasmere is one of the most popular villages in the Lakes.

The Best Full-Day Tours

Lake District in One Week

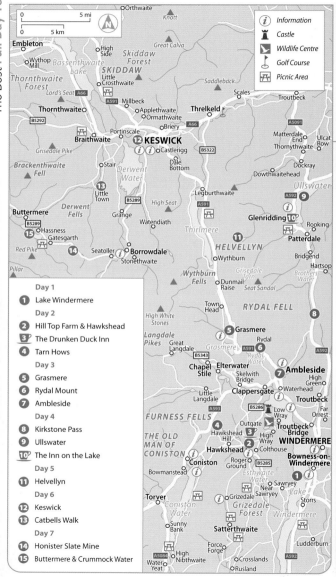

Map legend:
- (i) Information
- ♜ Castle
- ▼ Wildlife Centre
- ⛳ Golf Course
- 🎪 Picnic Area

0 — 5 mi
0 — 5 km

With a week in the Lake District, you will have time to settle into the Lake District's laid-back pace, relaxing on Windermere boat cruises, enjoying long, indulgent dinners of Cumbrian cuisine and leisurely visits to Lakeland villages. You might even decide to try something new, like walking up a mountain or traversing a rock face. It means your trip is less of a dash, so you can make photo stops on spectacular passes or relax on steamboat trips across Ullswater without having to cram everything into a couple of days. You might even want to book accommodation in more than one location; staying near the lakes of Windermere, Ullswater and Derwentwater means you have easy access to all the suggestions on this tour.

Day One

❶ Lake Windermere. Spend the first day exploring Windermere, including a boat trip, as described in ❶–❸ in the Long Weekend tour. *For a full tour of Bowness, see p 102.*

Day Two

❷ Hill Top Farm & Hawkshead. Start early to get to the front of the queue at **Beatrix Potter's former home**. Afterwards, spend the rest of the morning exploring Hawkshead village, as described in ❽ and ❾ of the Long Weekend tour on p 14.

Take a Break

❸ The Drunken Duck Inn. This family-owned pub is renowned for both its food and beer, which it brews on-site at the Barngates Brewery. The menu includes traditional British favourites with a modern twist. *Barngates, nr Ambleside.* ☎ *015394 36347. www.drunken duckinn.co.uk.*

❹ Tarn Hows. This is a small but very pretty lake bequeathed to the National Trust by Beatrix Potter along with other large areas of her estate. The woodland and fell views,

There are several places to visit on Lake Windermere Cruises.

Explore the rooms and gardens at Rydal Mount.

and **smooth pathways** around the lake that are wheelchair accessible, make it a popular beauty spot for the whole family. *For more information on the lake, see p 66.*

Day Three

5 Grasmere. You can park at **Dove Cottage and the Wordsworth Museum and Gallery** just outside Grasmere and then stroll into the village to explore other local attractions listed in **10** of the Long Weekend tour. *For detailed information on Grasmere, see p 114.*

6 Rydal Mount. Wordsworth's last home contains several rooms of memorabilia and has award-winning gardens. If you come here straight after lunch, you may find it less crowded. *For more information on Rydal Mount, see p 36,* **3***.*

7 Ambleside. You can pick up any outdoor equipment you need at the shops in Ambleside, and even find some bargains at Gaynor Sports. Take a short walk uphill from the Salutation Hotel (follow the path at the back or take the road alongside the Old Market Hall) to see the

It's a steep, winding road up to Kirkstone Pass.

90-foot waterfall **Stock Ghyll Force** and enjoy the real ales at Ambleside's lively pubs in the evening. *For more information on Ambleside's attractions, see p 96.*

Day Four

❽ **Kirkstone Pass.** This is the highest road in the Lake District with spectacular views across the region. If you don't have a car, it's worth taking the **Kirkstone Rambler bus** from Windermere or Troutbeck to Glenridding. If you're driving, take the steep Kirkstone Road out of Ambleside, a long and relentless uphill climb. Eventually it joins the A592 High Kingate road, where you can stop to take in the panoramic views and maybe stop for refreshment at the **Kirkstone Pass Inn.** Continue north along the road, and as you descend you'll catch sight of **Brothers Water**, a small lake beside the road. You can park here for more photo opportunities or continue downhill to Patterdale and Glenridding.

❾ **Ullswater.** Ullswater is the second-largest lake in the Lake District. Most tourist facilities are clustered at either end, around **Glenridding** and **Pooley Bridge**. From the small

Aira Force is located along a woodland trail.

Ullswater moves at a relaxing pace.

lakeside village of Glenridding, you can take an **Ullswater Steamer** boat to Howtown or Pooley Bridge, passing beautiful scenery at Barton Fell. Alternatively, follow trails around the south end of the lake through Patterdale, continuing along the east side of the lake if you want a longer walk. Return to Glenridding by boat. Pooley Bridge is a pretty enough tourist village with a couple of pubs and hotels. If you have time after your return, drive north along the A592 to **Aira Force**, a 70-foot high waterfall set within a woodland park. *For more information on the Ullswater area, see the East Lakes regional tour, p 70.*

Take a Break

 ❿ **The Inn on the Lake.** This hotel has a splendid setting overlooking Ullswater and the Helvellyn fells. Even if you're not staying here, you can still enjoy the Lake View Restaurant, which serves tasty dishes such as king scallop salad and loin of lamb. *Ullswater, Glenridding.* ☎ *017684 82444. www.lake districthotels.net. Hotel $$–$$$, restaurant $$$.*

You can buy gifts of all sizes at Honister Slate Mine.

Day Five

11 Helvellyn. The Lake District's third-highest peak can be tackled from several starting points. From Glenridding, it's a long but unforgettable walk across its famous razor-like ridge, **Striding Edge**. *For more walks, see Outdoors p 147.*

Day Six

12 Keswick. Its attractions include several museums, a variety of boat trips and the delightful Theatre by the Lake. See p 13, **5** of the Long Weekend tour. *For a full tour of Keswick, see p 128.*

13 Catbells Walk. This hill walk suits most fitness levels, challenging enough to push the inexperienced but not too long if you tire easily. As you climb, you'll see fabulous views of Derwentwater, with Castlerigg Fell opposite and Blencathra rising beyond Keswick. The most pleasant approach route to Catbells is via Hawes End (reached by boat); you can return from High Brandlehow afterwards. *For more information on Derwentwater boat trips and Catbells, see p 131 and p 150.*

The Maid of Buttermere

When Samuel Taylor Coleridge reported in the *London Morning Post* on the marriage of a country girl to a minor noble, little did he know that he was creating a legend. The Lakeland poet wasn't the only one to write about Mary Robinson, as William Wordsworth mentioned her in *Prelude*. But it was Joseph Palmer that first wrote about the Cumbrian beauty after his stay at the Inn in Buttermere, where her father was landlord, in 1792. Ten years later the still-unmarried Mary was duped by a passing fraudster, who introduced himself as Colonel Alexander Hope, brother of the Earl of Hopetoun. He married Mary within months, prompting Keswick correspondent Coleridge to write about the romance of it. Before long it emerged that Hope was actually a bigamist and bankrupt named John Hatfield. Hatfield was arrested, tried and hung, in 1803, while Mary won the heart of the public. Eventually she married a local farmer, Richard Harrison, and had four children. She died on February 7, 1937, but continues to inspire writers, including Melvyn Bragg whose novel *The Maid of Buttermere* (1987) was adapted for stage. The Inn remains, now called the Fish Hotel, Buttermere (☎ 017687 70253, www.fish-hotel.co.uk), and is still popular with anglers, walkers and climbers. Doubles from £96.

Deep in the Mountain

While most visitors come to tour the mine or enjoy the thrill of the *via ferrata* (see p 160), Honister still has a working mine and a craftsman using traditional techniques of docking, riving and dressing the slate to create 36-inch roofing tiles. It's thought that mining may have taken place here as far back as the Romans, but it really began in the mid 18th century with quarrying, followed by underground mines from 1833. Before 'inclines' were installed in 1879 to transport the slates away, packhorses followed the risky route up and down the mountain and all the way to the Cumbrian coast. Sleds were also used, with up to ⅓ of a ton of slate taken downhill by the barrow-men, who then unloaded the slate and transported the empty sled back uphill. After attempting the *via ferrata* route equipped with a hard-hat and climbing harness, I cannot imagine doing this in just a flat cap and shirtsleeves. As well as inclines, road, tram and train further facilitated transport, but this didn't stop the mine falling into decline, eventually closing in 1986. Ten years later, Mark Weir and Bill Taylor, descendents of two former miners, leased the mine and restarted the mine as a heritage enterprise.

Day Seven

⑭ Honister Slate Mine. High in Honister Pass, with superb views down into the valley below, this attraction offers one of the Lake District's most exciting experiences. Strap on a climbing harness and hard hat for the *via ferrata*, a system of cables and footholds set safely into the rock, which enables even those with no climbing experience to traverse the mountainside. Don't worry, you're accompanied every step of the way by an experienced and qualified climbing instructor. The younger or more timid can opt for a hard-hat mine tour, and experience the slate-miner's world in dripping darkness. *Honister Pass, Borrowdale. ☎ 017687 77230 for mine tours and general enquiries; ☎ 017687 77714 for Via Ferrata tickets. www.honister-slate-mine.co.uk, Admission Mine Tours*

£9.75 adults, £4.75 under 16yrs; Via Ferrata Classic £25 adults, £20 children; Via Ferrata Zip Wire £35 adults, £25 under 16yrs; All-day pass (mine tour, lunch and Via Ferrata) Classic £37 adults, £28 under 16yrs, £125 family (2+2); All-day Zip Wire £48 adults, £34 under 16yrs, £160 family. Open daily 9am–5pm. Transport Stagecoach Rambler 78.

⑮ Buttermere & Crummock Water. After the extreme experience of Honister, enjoy the peaceful drive down to Buttermere. If you have enough daylight and energy left, you can park at Gatesgarth and walk the few gentle miles around Buttermere or drive alongside the lake, passing Crummock Water, looping back through Whinlatter Forest Park. *For more information, see the North Lakes regional tour, p 78. Stagecoach Rambler 78.*

Lake District in **Two Weeks**

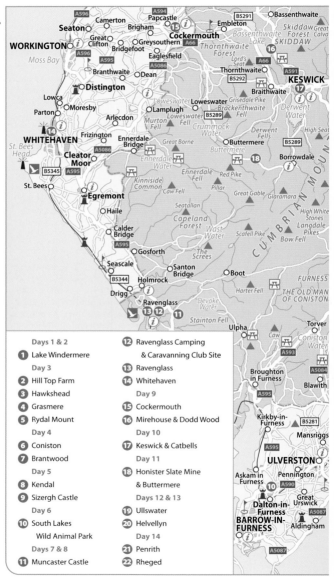

i	Information
♜	Castle
📐	Wildlife Centre
⊞	Picnic Area
⚑	Golf Course
⛯	Lighthouse

With two weeks in the Lake District, you can explore the fringes of the Lake District National Park such as Georgian Cockermouth, seafaring Whitehaven and haunted Muncaster Castle. It also gives you time to do what you really love, whether that is having down time close to your hotel, wandering through picturesque villages and shopping for typical Cumbrian crafts, or taking advantage of the watersports facilities, having a few adventures and maybe climbing a few fells. You should still have time to take in the best attractions in Kendal or Penrith.

Coniston's Ruskin Museum has an interesting collection of Cambell memorabilia.

Days One & Two

1 Lake Windermere. You can easily spend a couple of leisurely days exploring Windermere with boat trips, train rides, an aquarium, bicycle rides into **Grizedale Forest Park** and several attractions and shopping in **Bowness** and **Ambleside**. See **1**–**4** of the Long Weekend tour on p 12. Try and make time to see **Blackwell**, the Arts and Crafts house, superbly restored to show off Baillie Scott's late 19th-century architectural masterpiece. *For a full tour of Ambleside and Bowness, see p 96 and p 102, and for Blackwell, see p 65.*

Day Three

2 Hill Top Farm 3 Hawkshead 4 Grasmere & 5 Rydal Mount. Follow Day Three of the Long Weekend tour on p 14. If you don't start the day early or want to take things at a more leisurely pace, then choose two or three places to visit.

Day Four

6 Coniston. Coniston is small enough to explore in a couple of hours. The main attraction here is the **Ruskin Museum**, an eclectic collection of geology and mining displays, a boat owned by Arthur

Ransome, author of *Swallows and Amazons,* John Ruskin writings and drawings, and (from 2010), Donald Campbell's reconstructed *Bluebird K7.* Walk down to the marina on Coniston Water for boat trips around the lake and across to Brantwood. *For more information on Coniston and the Ruskin Museum, see p 110.*

7 Brantwood. The easiest way to come here is by boat, as the car park is quite small. The home of social thinker and art critic John Ruskin from 1872 until his death, Brantwood is a large house overlooking Coniston Water. Explore the house and garden trails, and relax with a coffee or lunch at the café. *For more information on Brantwood, see p 112. Coniston ☎ 015394 41396. www.brantwood.org.uk, Admission £5.95 adults; £4.50 students; £1.20 children; £4 gardens only; £11.95 family; there are also combined bus, boat and Brantwood tickets—ask at Coniston TIC or call ☎ 0871 2002233. Open mid-Mar–mid-Nov daily 11am–5.30pm; mid-Nov–mid-Mar daily 11.30am–4.30pm. Bus 505 from Windermere/Ambleside*

Art lovers won't want to miss Abbott Hall in Kendal.

to Coniston, then launch to Brantwood or Gondola (p 111) from Easter to Oct.

Day Five

8 Kendal. Often known as the Gateway to the Lakes, Kendal is a busy town that grew up on the wool industry. Today its former

Sizergh Castle was built in the Middle Ages.

Muncaster Great Hall.

tradesmen's yards are filled with modern shops. **Kendal Castle**, the **Museum of Lakeland Life** and the **Kendal Museum** trace its history. Other attractions include **The Quaker Tapestry** and **Abbott Hall Art Gallery**, while at night the **Brewery Arts Centre** is the place for entertainment. *For a full tour of Kendal, see p 122.*

9 Sizergh Castle. Try and leave a couple of hours to see this castle, which dates back to the Middle Ages. The surrounding gardens are filled with wild flowers and well-trimmed lawns. There are quizzes for kids, a shop and café. *For more information , see p 46,* **8**. *Sizergh, nr Kendal* ☎ *015395 60951. www. nationaltrust.org.uk. Admission £7.50 adults; £3.80 children; £18.80 family; garden only £4.90 adults; £2.50 children. Open mid-Mar–Oct castle Sun–Thurs 12pm–5pm; garden 11am–5pm. Bus 552, 555.*

Day Six
10 South Lakes Wild Animal Park. You could spend the best part of a day here, seeing lions, bears, rhinoceros and giraffes from a safe distance or getting closer to lemurs,

ostriches and wallabies. *For more information on the animal park, see p 57,* **4**. *Broughton Road, Dalton-in-Furness.* ☎ *01229 466086. www. wildanimalpark.co.uk, Admission £11.50 adults; £8 3–15 yrs and seniors; free under 3 yrs; £1.50 friends of the park. Open Easter–Nov daily 10am–5pm; Nov–Easter daily 10am–4.30pm. Train to Dalton-in-Furness; bus X9 from Bowness and Windermere.*

Days Seven & Eight
11 Muncaster Castle. Set on a large estate near Ravenglass, Muncaster Castle is owned and still occupied by the ancestral Pennington family. You'll see photos and portraits of them around the house, along with the court jester **Tom Fool**, who is said to haunt the place. You can spend a night here **ghost watching** if you wish. The **World Owl Centre** is located on the extensive grounds, which overlook the Eskdale Valley. *For more information on the castle and gardens, see p 42,* **3** *and p 57,* **5**. *Muncaster, nr Ravenglass* ☎ *01229 717614. www. muncaster.co.uk. Admission gardens, owl centre and maze £8 adults; £6 children 5–15 yrs; £26*

family; free under 5 yrs. Castle upgrade £x +£2.50 adults; +£1 children; +£4 family. Open mid-Mar–beginning Nov gardens, maze and owl centre daily 10.30am–6pm; castle Sun–Fri 12pm–4.30pm. Train to Ravenglass station (circa 1 mile).

⑫ Ravenglass Camping & Caravanning Club Site. Surrounded by woodland on the trail between Ravenglass and Muncaster Castle, this site is just a ten-minute stroll from the seafront and well placed for exploring the Cumbrian coast. *Ravenglass.* ☎ *01229 717250. www.siteseeker.co.uk.*

⑬ Ravenglass. A mile down the road from Muncaster Castle, Ravenglass is home to two railway lines, the steam-powered Ravenglass and Eskdale Railway and a mainline coastal route that's part of the National Rail network. A woodland walk leads from Ravenglass Camping and Caravanning Club Site past a Roman Bathhouse and on towards Muncaster. *For more information on Ravenglass, see the East Lakes and Coast tour, p 70.*

⑭ Whitehaven. You can drive or take the train to Whitehaven from Ravenglass. Adults and children can have fun here, exploring the town's past with interactive exhibits at The Beacon and The Rum Story museums. *For a full tour of Whitehaven, see p 144.*

Day Nine

⑮ Cockermouth. Just north of the Lake District National Park, Cockermouth has a handsome Georgian centre. Visit **Wordsworth's birthplace** and take a tour of **Jennings Brewery**, ending with a taste of their brews. *For a full tour of Cockermouth, see p 106.*

⑯ Mirehouse & Dodd Wood. Located beside Bassenthwaite Lake, Mirehouse is a family-run historic house open to the public in summer. In the grounds there are nature trails for kids and the Old Sawmill Tearoom, open for lunch and refreshments. Across the road is Dodd Wood (freely accessible), with more waymarked walks and an osprey viewing point. *Off the A591*

Keswick Launches zigzag across Derwentwater.

There are train trips through the Eskdale Valley from Ravenglass.

by Bassenthwaite Lake ☎ 017687 72287. www.mirehouse.com. Admission house and grounds £6 adults; £3 children; £17 family. Garden only £3 adults; £1.50 children. Open Apr–Oct house Wed and Sun (and Fri afternoon in Aug) 2pm–5pm; gardens, playgrounds, walks and tearooms daily 10am–5pm. Bus 74 from Keswick.

Day Ten

⑰ Keswick & Catbells. Spend the day enjoying Keswick's museums, theatre, boat trips and an afternoon walk up Catbells, as described in **⑤** and **⑦** of the Long Weekend tour. *For a full tour of Keswick, see p 128.*

Day Eleven

⑱ Honister Slate Mine & Buttermere. *Follow Day Seven of the One Week tour p 21.*

Days Twelve & Thirteen

⑲ Ullswater & ⑳ Helvellyn walk. Spend a couple of days taking boat trips, walking around Aira Force waterfall and along Lakeland paths, or to the peak of Helvellyn, as described in **⑨** and **⑪** of the One Week tour.

Day Fourteen

㉑ Penrith. On your last day, stroll round Penrith Castle before browsing the town's independent shops. At **㉒ Rheged** you'll find several products made in Cumbria under one roof, as well as activities, play areas and films for kids. *For a full tour of Penrith, see p 134.* ●

Beatrix Potter

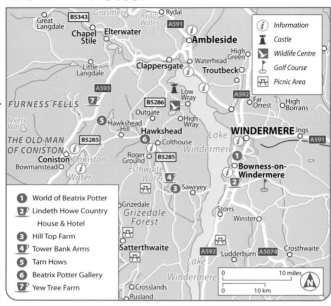

	Information
	Castle
	Wildlife Centre
	Golf Course
	Picnic Area

1 World of Beatrix Potter
2 Lindeth Howe Country House & Hotel
3 Hill Top Farm
4 Tower Bank Arms
5 Tarn Hows
6 Beatrix Potter Gallery
7 Yew Tree Farm

For decades, visitors have flocked to the Lakes from all over the world to pay homage to the children's author Beatrix Potter. Even more have arrived since the production of the film version of her life story. But you don't have to be an avid fan of Peter Rabbit and his friends to enjoy visiting the sights associated with her name. Kids love the fantastical World of Beatrix Potter; while Hill Top and Yew Tree Farm give a telling insight into Lakeland life. Tarn Hows (once owned by the author) is one of the prettiest of all the lakes in the area. START: **World of Beatrix Potter. Transport: bus 505, 516, 519, 541, 555; train to Windermere station.**

1 ★★ **World of Beatrix Potter.** This attraction might be aimed mainly at children (p 56, **1**), but fans of all ages can indulge themselves here. Models of the characters in carefully detailed settings bring the stories to life; Beatrix Potter books and a wide range of

Potteresque merchandise are on sale in the well-stocked shop. *Bowness-on-Windermere.* ☎ *015394 88444. www.hop-skip-jump.com. Admission £6 adults; £3 children. Open daily summer 10am–5.30pm; winter 10am–4.30pm.*

Mrs Tiggiewinkle at The World of Beatrix Potter™ Attraction.

Take a Break

2️⃣ Lindeth Howe Country House & Hotel.
Beatrix Potter spent family holidays here as a teenager. Later in life she became its owner. It's easy to see why she loved this house, with its lush grounds and lakeside views. Now run as a hotel, it has a leisure centre and a well-regarded restaurant serving locally sourced produce. *Lindeth Drive, Longtail Hill, Bowness-on-Windermere ☎ 015394 45759. www.lindeth-howe.co.uk. Doubles £160–£250. Restaurant open for lunch and dinner, menus £10.95–£39.95.*

3️⃣ ★★★ Hill Top Farm.
You're given a timed ticket to visit the house, and it's best to arrive early (before opening time) in peak periods to avoid the queues. From the ticket office, it's a five-minute walk up to the house.

There's nothing grand or glamorous about Hill Top, but this modest Lakeland house with its uncontrived cottage garden evokes the perfect setting for her characters and stories.

A gateway beside the shop leads through to the gardens, billowing with lilacs, herbs, fruit trees and butterflies all summer; it's no hardship to wait in these surroundings until the time for your tour. Inside the 17th-century stone house, things remain much as they were during the author's lifetime. Notice the paintings by her brother and plates decorated by her father. There's even a copy of the letter she wrote to Noel Moore, the sick son of her former governess, which formed the basis of *The Tale of Peter Rabbit. Near Sawrey, Hawkshead. ☎ 015394 36269. www.nationaltrust.org.uk. Admission £6.20 adult; £3.10 children; £15.50 family. Open house mid-Feb–mid-Mar Sat–Thurs 11am–3.30pm; mid-Mar–Oct Sat–Thurs 10.30am–4.30pm; garden mid-Feb–Mar daily 11am–4pm; first two weeks Mar and Nov–24 Dec daily 10am–4pm; mid-Mar–Oct daily 10.30am–5pm. Boat to Ferry House and walk; bus 525.*

Take a Break

4 Tower Bank Arms. As you walk from the National Trust car park/ticket office and Hill Top Farm you can't miss this typical 17th-century Lakeland inn, with its characteristic sentry box porch with a clock above. You can stop here for a meal made from freshly cooked local produce or sample one of the regional beers on tap. They also have a few guestrooms. *Near Sawrey, Hawkshead* ☎ *015394 36334. www.towerbankarms.co.uk/. Open peak season daily 11am–11pm; low season daily 11am–3pm and 5pm–11pm. Mains from £8.95.*

5 ★★ Tarn Hows. This quintessential Lakeland beauty spot, 2.5 miles from Hawkshead, is typical of the picturesque landscapes that Beatrix Potter bequeathed to the National Trust. Many of these lie between Hawkshead and Coniston. Easy trails fringe the shoreline, surrounded by woodland, mountain views and wildlife. In spring there are bluebells and in autumn the trees turn spectacular shades of red, gold and burnt orange. There are two small car parks, one for disabled visitors, and a viewing bench 300m away. *One mile north of the B5285 at High Cross, near Hawkshead. www.nationaltrust.org.uk. Bus X31.*

6 ★ Beatrix Potter Gallery. This building in the heart of picturesque Hawkshead village once housed the offices of Beatrix Potter's husband, William Heelis. Buy your tickets from the nearby box office then enter via the low gallery door. Inside, the 17th-century building is little changed, except for the collections of Potter illustrations and displays about her life. *Main Street, Hawkshead.* ☎ *015394 36355. www.nationaltrust.org.uk. Admission £4.20 adults; £2.10 children; £10.50 family. Open mid-Feb–mid-Mar Sat–Thurs 11am–3.30pm; mid-Mar–Oct 10.30am–4.30pm. Bus 505.*

Take a Break

7 Yew Tree Farm. This pretty B&B and working farm was once owned by Beatrix Potter and

Hill Top Farm, Beatrix Potter's Lake District home.

Yew Tree Farm, near Coniston, featured in the film Miss Potter.

featured as Hill Top Farm in the recent film about her life, *Miss Potter*. The cosy rooms here get booked up quickly, but you can take a break at the Tea Room, furnished by Beatrix Potter in 1930. The menu includes cream teas, cold salad buffets or hot meals such as Herdwick hot pot, chilli, and moussaka. If you want to take some Herdwick lamb home, you can buy this and other regional delights in the farm shop. *A593, Coniston, LA21 8DP* ☎ *015394 41433. www.yewtree-farm.com. Tearoom open Jun–Oct 11am–4pm.*

Beatrix Potter

Beatrix Potter was born on 28th July 1866 in Victorian London to wealthy parents, and was educated at home by several governesses. She developed an interest in nature and animals during family holidays in the Lake District, and began sketching and studying profusely. Her first book, *The Tale of Peter Rabbit,* was based on a tale she had sent to the sick son of her former governess. It was published by Frederick Warne & Co in 1902. She published another 22 illustrated books over the next 28 years.

Defying her parents' disapproval, Beatrix became secretly engaged to her publisher, Norman Warne, but soon afterwards he died tragically from a rare illness. With the proceeds of her books, Beatrix Potter bought Hill Top in Near Sawrey along with many other farms and large areas of land in the surrounding Lake District. She eventually married her solicitor, William Heelis, at the age of 47. An avid supporter of the countryside and a pioneer conservationist, she left most of her estate (4000 acres of land, cottages and 15 farms) to the National Trust. She died in Near Sawrey in 1943, aged 77, and her ashes were scattered nearby.

William Wordsworth & the **Lakeland Poets**

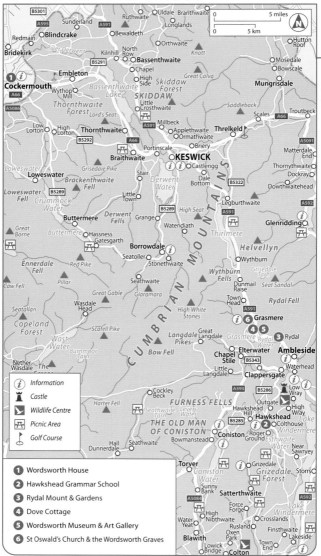

Legend:
- *i* Information
- Castle
- Wildlife Centre
- Picnic Area
- Golf Course

1. Wordsworth House
2. Hawkshead Grammar School
3. Rydal Mount & Gardens
4. Dove Cottage
5. Wordsworth Museum & Art Gallery
6. St Oswald's Church & the Wordsworth Graves

illiam Wordsworth's most famous lines of poetry are inextricably tied to the Lake District, particularly in spring when carpets of daffodils line the lakesides, grassy banks and gardens. This tour visits the places where he was born, lived, studied and wrote his best works, as well as his final resting place in the graveyard of St Oswald's Church in Grasmere. START: **Wordsworth House, Cockermouth. Transport: bus X4 to/from Keswick.**

William Wordsworth was born at Wordsworth House in Cockermouth.

❶ ★★★ Wordsworth House.

Now named after its most illustrious inhabitant, this elegant Georgian property was the Wordsworth family home and William's birthplace. His father, John Wordsworth, was a land agent for Sir William Lowther, who owned the property along with large chunks of what is now known as Cumbria. If you visit the house towards the end of the day there may not be so many visitors, but if you go earlier you might smell fresh bread being baked in the original kitchen by the Wordsworths' family cook.

Restored and owned by the National Trust, Wordsworth House is run as a living history recreation of a typical 1770s townhouse; you can meet and talk to the household 'servants' in period dress as you explore the house. The rooms have been painstakingly redecorated, using colour schemes, patterned wallpapers and traditional wooden furnishings typical of the time when William Wordsworth lived here. Outside, the garden has also been recreated to resemble its possible appearance during the late 18th century, with flowers, fruit trees, vegetables and herbs of the period. If it's a pleasant day, relax a while on one of the benches dotted around the pathways. *Main Street, Cockermouth.* ☎ *01900 820884. www.wordsworthhouse.org.uk. Admission £5.90 adults; £2.90 children; £14.70 family. Open Apr–Nov Mon–Sat 11am–5pm.*

Wordsworth's library at Rydal Mount.

2 ★★ Hawkshead Grammar School. It might be hard to imagine today, but this modest 400-year-old building was once one of the most prestigious grammar schools in the country, and certainly the best in the north of England. It was particularly renowned for mathematics. Pupils (all boys) also studied Latin and Greek, the younger ones downstairs and the older ones upstairs alongside the headmaster. Wordsworth was a pupil here for a time; you can see his name carved into one of the ground-floor desks, although there's no definite proof that he actually carved it.

The well-informed guide gives an interesting insight into the school's daily routine, both before and after Wordsworth's time, including methods of corporal punishment. In those days the boys smoked and drank weak beer (then regarded as safer than water). Upstairs you can see some of the books they studied. The school closed in 1909 but was used as an extra classroom until the

1950s. *Hawkshead.* ☎ *015394 36735. www.hawksheadgrammar. org.uk. Admission £2. Open Apr–Oct Mon–Sat 10am–1pm and 2pm–5pm (Oct until 3.30pm); Sun 1pm–5pm; closed Nov–Mar. Bus 555 to Ambleside/505 to Hawkshead.*

3 ★★★ Rydal Mount & Gardens. Wordsworth moved into Rydal Mount with his wife, Mary, sister Dorothy and daughter Dora in 1813. It remained the family home until Mary died in 1859, nine years after William's own death. Inside, you can see William's favourite 'cutlass' chair (designed for men with swords to sit in), along with family portraits and a noteworthy mezzotint of Robert Burns, for whom Wordsworth had great admiration. Upstairs in William and Mary's bedroom, there's a portrait of Queen Victoria, given to him by the Queen when he became Poet Laureate in 1843. You can also visit the bedrooms of Wordsworth's daughter Dora and his sister Dorothy. Like her brother, Dorothy was a gifted writer and lover of the Lakeland countryside. Her journals make fascinating reading.

Don't miss the study added by Wordsworth, with views across the gardens, which have been maintained almost exactly as Wordsworth designed them (p 44, ❷). Take the terrace steps to the left of the house and walk along the pathway to The Poet's Summerhouse. From here you can see Rydal Water and Dora's Field, planted with daffodils in memory of his beloved daughter, who died at the age of 43. *Rydal, near Ambleside, LA22 9LU* ☎ *015394 33002. www.rydalmount. co.uk. Admission £6 adults; £5 seniors and students; £4 garden only; £2.50 children 5–15 years; £15 family. Open Mar–Oct daily 9.30am–5pm; winter Wed–Sun 11am–4pm. Bus 505 to Ambleside, 555 to Rydal.*

❹ ★★★ **Dove Cottage.** Dove Cottage was Wordsworth's home from 1799–1808. This is the most popular of Wordsworth's homes with many visitors, and probably his

Wordsworth wrote some of his best poetry at Dove Cottage.

own favourite. The years he spent here during his early marriage were among the happiest and most creative of his life, when he wrote

William Wordsworth's desk at Rydal Mount.

William Wordsworth

Born in Cockermouth on 7th April 1770, William was introduced to poetry by his father at a young age. He attended **Hawkshead Grammar School** (see p 36, ②) for several years, continuing his studies at Cambridge University. Together with **Samuel Coleridge**, he published *Lyrical Ballads*, a seminal work of English Romantic poetry, in 1798. The following year, Wordsworth moved to Dove Cottage in Grasmere with his sister Dorothy. He married Mary Hutchinson in 1802, and together they had five children, two of them dying in infancy. Besides poetry, Wordsworth also wrote about travel, philosophy and politics (influenced by his walking tour of Europe, particularly revolutionary France), topics reflected in his long autobiographical work *The Prelude*, which was published shortly after his death. Wordsworth knew many of the artists and writers of his time, including Coleridge, and his brother-in-law **Robert Southey**; together, the three of them became known as the **Lake Poets**. After Southey died in 1843, Wordsworth became **Poet Laureate**, but his creative genius was deeply affected by the death of his daughter, Dora, in 1847. He died on 23rd April 1850 at the twelfth stroke of midnight.

those famous lines, 'I wandered lonely as a cloud…'.

Dove Cottage is small, and visitors initially have to join a timed tour, but you can then explore further at your leisure. Little is known of the house's origins, except that it was built around the early 17th century. During the 18th century it became an inn called the

The Wordsworth Museum is next to Dove Cottage.

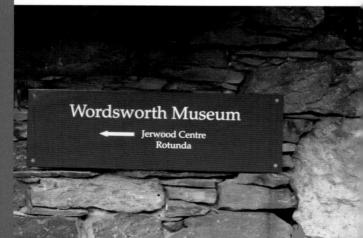

The Wordsworth family graves in St Oswald's Church cemetery, Grasmere.

Dove and Olive. At first Wordsworth lived here with his sister, Dorothy, but when he married, his wife Mary joined him, and three of their children (John, Dora and Thomas) were born here.

Downstairs, the rooms are quite snug, with little natural light and a cold pantry. Upstairs, the study and bedrooms get more daylight. The tour guide will point out various interesting items, including two portraits of Wordsworth, and the cutlass chair in which he used to write.

As the Wordsworth family expanded, they outgrew Dove Cottage, moving first to Allan Bank, (also in Grasmere), in 1808. This house is owned by the National Trust but is privately rented and not open to the public. *See below.*

❺ ★★ Wordsworth Museum & Art Gallery. This museum was founded by former poet laureate John Masefield in 1936. It houses works by some of the greatest exponents of this period of English literature and art, including watercolours and manuscripts. It also presents a packed programme of temporary exhibitions that take a fresh approach to Romanticism, drawing on both the permanent collection and borrowed material. *A591 at Town End.* ☎ *015394 35544. www.wordsworth.org.uk. Admission includes cottage and gallery £7.50 adults; £4.50 children; free under 6 yrs; £17.50 family (1–2 adults, 1–3 children). Open daily 9.30am–5.30pm (last admission 5pm). Bus 555.*

❻ ★ St Oswald's Church & the Wordsworth Graves. The Wordsworth family graves are in a peaceful setting overlooking the River Rothay. They include the graves of William and Mary Wordsworth, their daughter Dora and various other members of the family. Next to the churchyard is the Wordsworth Daffodil Garden, and inside the church there's a Wordsworth memorial. *Church Stile. Open daily 9am–5pm. Bus 555.*

Best Houses & Gardens

Information

Castle

Wildlife Centre

1 Mirehouse

2 Rydal Mount & Gardens

3 Muncaster Castle & Gardens

4 Holker Hall & Gardens

5 Holker Hall

6 Brantwood

7 Blackwell

8 Sizergh Castle & Gardens

9 Levens Hall

Haunted castles, mansions passed through generations of families and quintessential English gardens with croquet lawns, topiary and rose beds define some of the Lake District's most spectacular properties. This tour visits Elizabethan Levens Hall and 13th-century Muncaster Castle, which were built way before the Lake Poets popularized the region during the early 19th century. But you can also take in Wordsworth's own garden at Rydal Mount and Blackwell, an Arts and Crafts house with carefully crafted interiors.
START: **Mirehouse. Transport: bus: 554.**

❶ ★★ **Mirehouse.** Kids love this historic house with its woodland trails and **adventure playgrounds**. They can jump across streams, swing in big tyres, find their way around the **heather maze** or spot red squirrels on the Family Nature trail.

Tucked away on the east side of Bassenthwaite Lake, Mirehouse was built by the Earl of Derby in 1666. Today the **historic house** and estate is open to the public. One of the principal attractions inside the house is an important collection of works by **Francis Bacon** and letters from various authors and artists of international renown, such as William Wordsworth and John Constable.

Outside, the gardens have been transformed from tangled undergrowth into a stunning haven for wildlife and bees. Follow the circular walk through the **rhododendron tunnel** down to the banks of the lake. You can stop for refreshments or lunch in the **Old Sawmill tearoom**. *Off the A591 by Bassenthwaite Lake ☎ 017687 72287. www.mirehouse.com. Admission house and grounds £6 adults; £3 children; £17 family; garden only £3 adults; £1.50 children. Open Apr–Oct house Wed and Sun (and Fri afternoon in Aug) 2pm–5pm; gardens, playgrounds, walks and tearooms daily 10am–5pm. Bus 74 from Keswick.*

❷ ★★★ **Rydal Mount & Gardens.** Rydal Mount was Wordsworth's home from 1813 until his death in 1850. It was originally a yeoman's cottage, dating from the late 16th century. You can still recognize the original parts of the house by the low ceilings and beams. During the 18th century, it was transformed into a larger and grander family house.

The garden is the crowning glory, a lush green oasis where paths flow smoothly through lawns, flower-beds, shrubberies and woodland glades to the terraces by the house. Wordsworth's summer house is a peaceful retreat where he perfected his poetry. The carefully tended trees and shrubs include different kinds of maple, holly, cypress

Mirehouse is located beside Bassenthwaite Lake.

You can see Rydal Water from the shade of Wordsworth's peaceful summer house.

wand magnolia. In summer you can enjoy tea outside. *Rydal, near Ambleside, LA22 9LU ☎ 015394 33002. www.rydalmount.co.uk. Admission £6 adults; £5 seniors and students; £4 garden only; £2.50 children 5–15 years; £15 family. Open Mar–Oct daily 9.30am–5pm; winter Wed–Sun 11am–4pm. Bus 555.*

❸ ★★★ Muncaster Castle & Gardens. The World Owl Trust, (a conservation charity for the protection of owls) is based at Muncaster. Visitors can enjoy close encounters with many different species including barn, tawny and long-eared owls.

The castle itself is a grand residence continuously occupied by the Pennington family since the early 13th century. Inside the house, pictures and photographs of the family through the centuries include a rather unnerving clown-like portrait of Tom Skelton, better known as Tom Fool, a court jester at Muncaster in the 16th century.

Many spooky tales involve Tom Fool, who is said to haunt Muncaster Castle. Overnight guests tell of disturbed nights in the Tapestry Room, with echoing footsteps and turning door handles. You may feel a shiver down your spine in that room. *Muncaster, nr Ravenglass ☎ 01229 717614. www.muncaster.co.uk. Admission gardens, owl centre and maze £8 adults; £6 children 5–15 yrs; £26 family; free under 5 yrs. Castle upgrade £x +£2.50 adults; +£1 children; +£4 family. Open mid-Mar–beginning Nov gardens, maze and owl centre daily 10.30am–6pm; castle Sun–Fri 12pm–4.30pm. Train to Ravenglass station (circa 1 mile). Bus X6.*

Muncaster Castle is an impressive sight.

A large wing of Holker Hall was rebuilt in the 19th century following a devastating fire.

Coachman's Quarters. For the full Muncaster Experience, you can stay at the Coachman's Quarters in the castle grounds. These converted outbuildings offer flexible bed-and-breakfast accommodation suitable for families. ☎ *0845 4506445. www.penningtonhotels.com. Doubles £66–80.*

❹ ★★ Holker Hall & Gardens. Home to Lord and Lady Cavendish, Holker Hall is filled with family portraits.

Built in the early 16th century, it was taken over by the Cavendish family in 1756, when George Augustus, second son of the 3rd Duke of Devonshire, inherited the property from his cousin Sir William Lowther (p 35, ❶). The property came back to the 5th Duke of Devonshire and remained in their hands until the 9th Duke passed it onto his younger brother in the early 20th century; it is his descendents that live there today. The West Wing was destroyed in a devastating fire in 1871, but the 7th Duke rebuilt a grand red sandstone replacement in Elizabethan Gothic style, and this part is now open to the public.

Each room is filled with treasures: hundreds of tomes in the library; the original silk wallpaper in the drawing room; Chippendale tables and notable 18th-century landscape paintings from Sir William Lowther's collection. Upstairs there are several luxurious bedrooms, one named after Queen Mary, who stayed here in 1937.

The extensive grounds include formal Victorian gardens, woodland and 200 acres of parkland. *Cark-in-Cartmell* ☎ *01539 558328. www.*

The trees at Muncaster turn an array of colours in autumn.

Fool of Muncaster

Every year, Muncaster Castle holds the Festival of Fools, a five-day event with magic workshops, stand-up comedians and performance artists. The highlight, though, is the International Jester Tournament to elect the Fool of Muncaster.

holker-hall.org.uk. Admission hall and gardens £10 adults; £9 seniors and students; £5.50 children 6–15 yrs; £27.50 family; garden only £6.50 adults; £5.50 seniors and students; £3.50 children 6–15 years; £16.50 family. Open hall mid-Mar–Oct Sun–Fri 11am–4pm; gardens Sun–Fri 10.30am–5.30pm.

Take a Break

5 Holker Hall. The hall has two restaurants, the Burlington Room, where you can enjoy a traditional Sunday lunch, and the Cavendish Room, serving traditional British food, much of which comes from the estate. If you'd like to take some of the produce home, chutneys, paté and venison are on sale in the food hall. *Gift shop, restaurant and food hall. Open Feb–24 Dec daily 10.30am–5.30pm (4pm low season; 12pm on 24 Dec).*

6 ★★ Brantwood. This fine house on the banks of Coniston Water was the former home of art critic and **social philanthropist John Ruskin** from 1872–1900.

A visit to the house usually begins with a short film about Ruskin's life and the reasons for his move to Brantwood. The rest of the house reveals an intriguing collection of paintings, period furniture and personal treasures belonging to Ruskin. Although many of Ruskin's belongings were auctioned off after his death, his study is much the same as it was when he died, except for the piles of papers and books that once cluttered the floor. There are also rooms filled with Ruskin's own watercolours and sketches, and in his former bedroom upstairs the walls are lined with prints of Turner paintings (the 36 originals he had here were also sold).

Beyond Holker Hall's formal gardens are acres of parkland.

John Ruskin lived at Brantwood for 28 years.

Outside, the vast 250-acre property includes 15 acres of gardens with panoramic views of Coniston Water and the fells on the western side of the lake. *Coniston ☎ 015394-41396. www.brantwood.org.uk. Admission £5.95 adults; £4.50 students; £1.20 children; £4 gardens only; £11.95 family; there are also combined bus, boat and Brantwood tickets—ask at Coniston TIC or call ☎ 08712002233. Open mid-Mar–mid-Nov daily 11am–5.30pm; mid-Nov–mid-Mar daily 11.30am–4.30pm. Bus 505 from Windermere/Ambleside to Coniston, then launch to Brantwood or Gondola (p 141, ④) from Easter to Oct.*

❼ ★★★ Blackwell. Blackwell is an outstanding example of the Arts and Crafts style of architecture and interior design. Built by **MH Baillie Scott** between 1898 and 1900, it was rescued from dereliction by the Lakeland Arts Trust in the 1990s and restored to its present glory.

The exterior is painted white and decorated with numerous floral motifs (notice the drainpipes!) The rooms lead off a wood-panelled corridor—look out for the John Ruskin paintings. All around the Main Hall are reminders of the natural world: carved tulips on wooden doors, panels of painted flowers and a

The White Drawing Room contrasts sharply with the dark wood of the Great Hall.

Even the drains have been carefully designed.

peacock mosaic above the door leading to the Dining Room. The stark White Drawing Room makes a sharp contrast with the florid style elsewhere, but even here the theme continues with foliage patterns inlaid into doors and stained-glass windows. The centrepiece is the fireplace, where brilliant blue tiles stand out against the white walls as if reflecting the waters of Windermere, which can be seen through the window.

The trust wasn't sure about the decor of the bedroom but has

Blackwell has superb views of Lake Windermere.

decorated it simply as it thinks it might have been, brought to life by William Morris textiles. *Bowness-on-Windermere, B5360 (just off the B5074). ☎ 015394 46139. www. blackwell.org.uk. Admission £6.95 adults; £4.10 children and students; £18.50 family. Open daily 10.30am–5pm (closes two weeks early Jan).*

⑧ ★★ Sizergh Castle & Gardens. Built by the Strickland family during the Middle Ages, the castle is still occupied by their descendants today, although it's now managed by the National Trust. The house was extended in Elizabethan times and displays fine oak-panelled rooms, exceptional carved overmantles, family portraits and antique furniture. As you walk through the house, you can chat to the staff. Family portraits of Walter Strickland (1647–56) in **The Queens Room**, marked The Master 'JH' are thought to have been painted by Dom **Jerome Hesketh**, a priest who visited Roman Catholic households in the guise of a portrait artist to say Mass in secret.

Visiting children are given quizzes, encouraging them to notice seashell embellishments and other details in the paintings around the castle. Another takes them on a discovery trail around the garden, inevitably ending with ice cream at the café. Sizergh-related gifts and local crafts are on sale at the shop. *Sizergh, nr Kendal ☎ 015395 60951. www.nationaltrust.org.uk. Admission £7.50 adults; £3.80 children; £18.80 family; garden only £4.90 adults; £2.50 children. Open mid-Mar–Oct castle Sun–Thurs 12pm–5pm; garden 11am–5pm. Bus 552, 555.*

⑨ ★ Levens Hall. First built as a medieval pele tower, Levens Hall was later extended into a mansion with oak panelling and Italian plasterwork (you can still see Elizabeth

Sizergh Castle has a mixture of formal and wild flower gardens.

I's coat of arms in the drawing room). Colonel James Grahme took over the house in 1688, adding the impressive formal gardens, which still retain their original design, notably a splendid display of carefully tended topiary. There's also a small orchard and a herb garden. Today, Levens Hall is owned and run by the Bagot family. It contains many fascinating antiques and curiosities, such as two of the oldest pistols in England (above the fireplace in the entrance hall) and the Duke of Wellington's campaign bed.

At The Bellingham Buttery, you can try produce from the large estate attached to Levens Hall, including deer, goats, sea trout and salmon, plus its famous home-brewed Morocco Ale. *Levens Hall (off A6/ A590)* ☎ *015395 60321. www. levenshall.mullindesign.com. Admission house and gardens £10.50 adults; £4.50 children; £26 families; garden only £7.50 adults; £3.50 children; £19.50 family. Open early Apr–early Oct Sun–Thurs house 12pm–4.30pm; gardens and gift shop 10am–5pm. Bus 552, 555.*

Levens Hall was first built as a medieval pele tower.

Lake District **for Foodies**

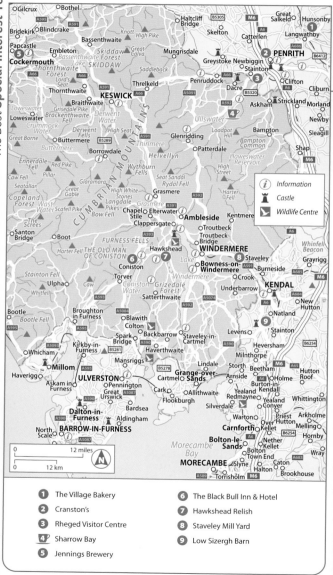

Information

Castle

Wildlife Centre

① The Village Bakery

② Cranston's

③ Rheged Visitor Centre

④ Sharrow Bay

⑤ Jennings Brewery

⑥ The Black Bull Inn & Hotel

⑦ Hawkshead Relish

⑧ Staveley Mill Yard

⑨ Low Sizergh Barn

Toe Lake District is renowned for good food. Local bakeries and micro-breweries, food halls and many excellent restaurants make the most of the region's excellent local produce. Below
are a few of my favourites: Staveley's range of independent food
stores, Low Sizergh Barn farm shop and Cranston's butchers. If you're
staying for a week or two, you can seek out micro-breweries and
individual food producers across the Lake District. START: **Melmerby.**
Transport: bus 130, 139, 888.

1 ★★ The Village Bakery. The
first time I came to this amazing
café-bakery in a tiny village, I had
just free-wheeled down hairpin
bends on my bicycle from Hartside,
a fell with spectacular views of the
east Cumbrian countryside. After a
blustery ride, I needed a hot cup of
tea and an indulgent slice of cake.
The smell of freshly baked, organic
bread and cakes fills the air as you
approach one of the best independent bakeries in the country. You
can buy many different kinds of
bread, often still hot from the oven,
all made with organic products
with varieties catering for special
dietary requirements. It used to be
baked on-site but these days the
bread is cooked in nearby Lazonby
and whisked over to Melmerby.
The on-site ovens are still used for
baking the cakes and granola for
breakfast.

The organic restaurant (Café vB)
serves breakfast and a seasonal menu
of classic British favourites: bacon,
sausage and egg breakfasts, or steak
and kidney pie. *Melmerby A686, nine
miles northeast of Penrith.* ☎ *017688
81811. www.village-bakery.com, Open
Mon–Thurs 8.30am–5pm, Sun and
bank holidays 9.30am–5pm.*

2 ★ Cranston's. At this Penrith
butchers, you can buy traditional
spiral-shaped Cumberland sausages; a single one can feed a family
of four or more! They also sell other
local meat, as well as picnic items
like fresh bread and ham, homemade coleslaw, fruit and ginger
beer. *Ullswater Road, Penrith, just
off M6 at J40.* ☎ *017688 68680.
www.cranstons.net. Open Tues
2pm–6pm; Wed–Sun 10am–6pm.*

3 ★★ Rheged Visitor Centre.
This one-stop shopping and

The Taste Farm Shop has a wide range of local produce.

Kids love Rheged whatever the weather.

entertainment centre carved into a hillside near Penrith enables you to have a meal or snack, buy some gifts and keep the kids amused (p 59, ⑨). The multi-galleried mall contains several food outlets, including Saunders Chocolates and the Taste Farm Shop, which stocks beer, juices, pickles, jams, chocolates and other tasty items from all over the Lakes. *Junction of A66 and A592.* ☎ *017688 68000. www.rheged.com. Admission giant movies £4.95 adults; £3.95 concessions; £3 children 5–15 yrs; £14 family (2 adults and 3 children);*

Jennings Brewery.

outdoor play £1.50 per child; indoor soft play free–£2.50 per hour under 6mths–over 1 yr.

Take a Break

④ **Sharrow Bay.** You'll need to dress smartly to dine at the Michelin-starred restaurant in this country-house hotel. Dine on dishes like fried fillet of plaice with shallot mash or medallion of veal with buttered spinach, sautéed and wild mushroom sauce! If your budget doesn't stretch to dinner, you could always try a light lunch or afternoon tea. Booking essential. *Ullswater* ☎ *01768 486301. One sitting 12.30pm for 1pm lunch, 7.30pm for 8pm dinner, and 4pm afternoon tea.*

⑤ ★★ **Jennings Brewery.** Brewery tours start with an introductory film about the history of the brewery and end with a half-pint. In between, you'll be taken through the whole brewing process, sample some barley grains and smell the hops. Needless to say, the products are on sale in the shop. *Cockermouth.* ☎ *0845 129 7185. www. jenningsbrewery.co.uk. Admission*

Cumbrian Breweries

Cumbria has 26 independent breweries—some occupy large purpose-built sites like Hawkshead Brewery in Staveley Mill Yard or Jennings Brewery in Cockermouth, others are micro-breweries on a much smaller scale, producing their brews at the back of a pub, for instance, Coniston Brewery at The Black Bull Inn and Hotel. The following websites supply useful information for real-ale connoisseurs about the breweries and beer events in Cumbria: www.cumbrian breweries.org.uk and www.cumbriacamra.org.uk. Camra (Campaign for Real Ale) has several supporting pubs in and around the Lake District where you can sample a range of award-winning beers. Try the Golden Rule in Ambleside (Smithy Brow. ☎ 015394 32257. Open daily 11am–11pm), which claims to serve the widest range of Camra-approved beers in Cumbria.

£5.50 adults; £2.50 children (over 12 yrs only). Open Tues 2pm–6pm; Wed–Sun 10am–6pm. Bus X4/5, 600.

❻ ★★ The Black Bull Inn & Hotel. Behind Coniston's Black Bull Inn is one of the Lake District's most celebrated micro-breweries, the **Coniston Brewing Company**. Whether or not you're staying at the inn, do try to visit the pub for dinner and a pint or two. Best known for ales such as Bluebird Bitter and Old

Man Ale, the brewery also produces a creamy, black stout. After hearing what I thought were dubious claims that it was better than Guinness, I joined my Irish husband in testing the claim. It certainly won our vote that night anyway. *Yewdale Road, Coniston. ☎ 015394 41335. www.conistonbrewery.com, Pub opening times daily 10am–11pm (food 12pm–9pm). Bus 505, X12.*

You can take a tour of Jennings Brewery.

Sample some local ales at The Black Bull in Coniston.

7 ★ Hawkshead Relish. I stumbled across this shop while strolling through pretty Hawkshead village and bought a selection of **mustard, chutney and jam** to take home. These hand-made products (which don't contain any artificial preservatives) are widely on sale elsewhere, however; you'll spot the distinctive black-and-white labels in speciality food shops everywhere from Low

Hawkshead Relish sells a range of hand-made pickles and chutneys.

Sizergh to Rheged. But there's a better choice at the Hawkshead shop, where you can pick'n'mix from their range and they'll pack your purchases in a special box. *The Square, Hawkshead.* ☎ *015394 36614. www.hawksheadrelish.com. Open Mon–Sat 9.30am–5.30pm; Sun 10am–5pm. Bus 505.*

8 ★★★ Staveley Mill Yard. Staveley Mill Yard is a foodie's heaven. At **Lucy Cooks** (☎ 015394 32288, www.lucycooks.co.uk/) you can take one-day courses in anything from cooking with an Aga to meals for kids and dinner parties. Find the perfect wine to accompany your new-found gastronomic talents from **Organico**, the largest organic wine shop in the UK (☎ 015398 22200, www.organi.co.uk). **More** (☎ 015398 22297, www.more artisan.co.uk) cooks fresh, artisan bread, desserts and chocolate that are quickly racking up plates of awards. At **Friendly Food and Drink** (☎ 015398 22326, www. friendlyfoodanddrink.co.uk), you can pick up handmade chutneys, sauces and jams. After all that

Sweet Treats

The **Grasmere Gingerbread Shop** (☎ 015394 35428, www.grasmeregingerbread.co.uk) is famous for its gingery cakes. One of my favourite sweetshops is **Ye Olde Friars** (☎ 017687 72234, www.friarsofkeswick.co.uk) with sweets and chocolates piled high around the shop. In Penrith, **The Toffee Shop** (☎ 01768 862008, www.thetoffeeshop.co.uk) sells mouthwatering fudge and toffee, while kids love **Abbott Lodge Jersey Ice Cream** (p 60, ⑩, ☎ 01931 712720, www.abbottlodgejerseyeyicecream.co.uk) and **Wellington Jersey Ice Cream** (☎ 01900 822777, www.wellingtonjerseys.co.uk) at Cockermouth. You'll find more sweet and savoury goodies at Farmers' Markets—for more information, see Savvy Traveler p 183.

thirsty work, you can take a tour of **Hawkshead Brewery** (☎ 015398 22644 hawksheadbrewery.co.uk) and sample some of their brews in the Beer Hall. **Wilf's Café** (☎ 015398 22329, www.wilfs-cafe.co.uk) is a great place for continental or full English breakfasts, soups and salad, and speciality food evenings. Or just cool off with **Scoops Ice Cream** (☎ 015398 22866, www.scoopchocice.co.uk) and chocolates made from Sizergh Low Barn's organic milk by a well-known firm called The Windermere Ice Cream and Chocolate Company. *Staveley Mill Yard.* ☎ *015398 21234. http://www.staveleymillyard.com. Open various. Train to Staveley station.*

⑨ ★★ Low Sizergh Barn. I return to this enticing **shop and café** almost every time I visit the Lake District. The shop on the ground floor sells a wide range of locally produced vegetables, meat, pickles and other items, including a few from farther afield. Upstairs, the café is a great pit-stop for a pot of tea, accompanied by an irresistible choice of mouthwatering cakes. If you time your tea break right, you

might get a birds-eye view of the cows as they're brought in for afternoon milking. If you want to explore further, there's a mile-long trail around the farm from the far end of the car park. *Low Sizergh Farm, Sizergh, nr Kendal.* ☎ *015395 60426. www.lowsizerghbarn.co.uk. Open Easter-Dec shop daily 9am-5.30pm; tea room daily 9.30am-5pm; 2 Jan-Easter shop daily 9am-5pm; tea room daily 9.30am-4.45pm.*

Sarah Nelson opened her Grasmere shop in the 19th century.

Lake District **with Kids**

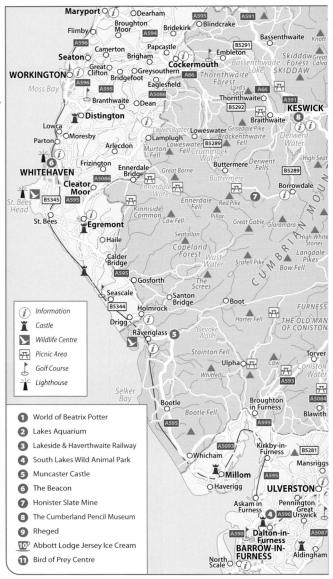

Maryport
Dearham
Broughton Moor
Bridekirk
Blindcrake
A595
Bassenthwaite
Knott
Flimby
A594
B5291
Embleton
Skiddaw Great
Forest Calva
SKIDDAW
Seaton
Camerton
Papcastle
Brigham
Cockermouth
Bassenthwaite Lake
Great Clifton
Greysouthern
A66
Thornthwaite Forest
WORKINGTON
Bridgefoot
A5086
Lord's Seat
A66
Thornthwaite
A591
KESWICK
Moss Bay
A596
A595
Eaglesfield
Dean
B5292
8
Branthwaite
Braithwaite
Distington
Lorton
Loweswater
Loweswater
Grisedale Pike
Derwent
Water
Lowca
Moresby
Lamplugh
Brackenthwaite Fell
Parton
6
Arlecdon
Murton Fell
Loweswater
Crummock Water
B5289
Buttermere
Derwent Fells
High Seat
WHITEHAVEN
Frizington
Ennerdale Bridge
A5086
Great Borne
Buttermere
Red Pike
Borrowdale
B5289
Cleator Moor
Ennerdale Water
Ennerdale Fell
Pillar
Great Gable
7
Glaramara
CUMBRIAN MOUN
St. Bees Head
B5345
A595
Kinniside Common
Caw Fell
High White Stones
St. Bees
Egremont
Seatallan
Copeland Forest
Wast Water
Scafell Pike
Langdale Pikes
Bow Fell
Haile
Calder Bridge
A595
Gosforth
The Screes
FURNESS
THE OLD MAN OF CONISTON
Seascale
B5344
Santon Bridge
Boot
Harter Fell
Torver
Coniston Water
Holmrock
Drigg
Ravenglass
5
Devoke Water
Ulpha
Caw
A593
Whitfell
Stainton Ground
A5084
Selker Bay
Bootle
Bootle Fell
A595
Broughton in Furness
A595
Blawith
A5093
Kirkby-in-Furness
B5281
Mansriggs
Whicham
Millom
A595
ULVERSTON
Haverigg
Askam in Furness
4
A590
Pennington
Great Urswick
A5087
North Scale
Dalton-in-Furness
BARROW-IN-FURNESS
Aldingham

Legend:
- *i* Information
- Castle
- Wildlife Centre
- Picnic Area
- Golf Course
- Lighthouse

1. World of Beatrix Potter
2. Lakes Aquarium
3. Lakeside & Haverthwaite Railway
4. South Lakes Wild Animal Park
5. Muncaster Castle
6. The Beacon
7. Honister Slate Mine
8. The Cumberland Pencil Museum
9. Rheged
10. Abbott Lodge Jersey Ice Cream
11. Bird of Prey Centre

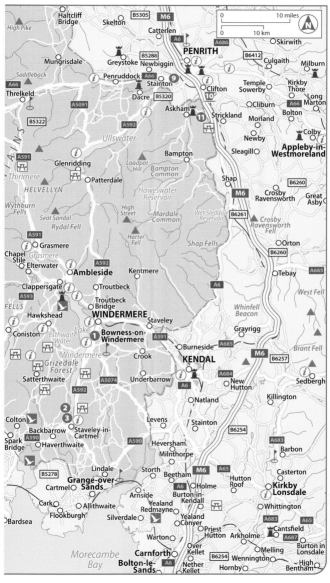

The animal kingdom is usually a big winner as a family attraction, and in the Lake District you can see creatures of the deep at the Lakes Aquarium, lazy lions at the South Lakes Animal Park and even hold an eagle at the Bird of Prey Centre. If it's raining, it's easy to forget about the weather with indoor favourites such as Rheged discovery centre's six-floor-high cinema screen, The Beacon's hands-on exploration of Whitehaven life and Honister Slate Mine's tour inside the mountain. Several of the attractions below have trails and quizzes for kids too, including Muncaster Castle and The Cumberland Pencil Museum. START: **World of Beatrix Potter, Bowness-on-Windermere. Transport: bus 505, 516, 519, 555, X8, X9; train to Windermere station.**

❶ ★★ **World of Beatrix Potter.** Younger visitors are given a pair of rabbit ears as they enter this appealing wet-weather attraction. After watching a short film, you walk round an indoor gallery flanked by detailed tableaux of scenes from the Beatrix Potter tales, with large models of Peter Rabbit, Mrs Tiggy-Winkle, Squirrel Nutkin, Tom Thumb, Hunker Munker and their friends. Each vitrine is accompanied by text from the books, and the dimmed lighting, scented air and music enhance the fantasy. Designed for younger children, it's a trip down memory lane for quite a few adults too. *Bowness-on-Windermere.* ☎ *015394 88444.*

The World of Beatrix Potter is a favourite with younger children and Potter fans alike.

www.hop-skip-jump.com. Admission £6 adults; £3 children. Open daily summer 10am–5.30pm; winter 10am–4.30pm. Bus: 505, 516, 555, X8, X9.

❷ ★★ **Lakes Aquarium.** This attraction provides a fascinating insight into marine life for all ages, but some of the interactive exhibits will be particularly appealing to children. From reception, you follow a route round the aquarium, passing a tank full of huge carp before passing through a three-tiered glass tunnel full of fish and small creatures found under Lake Windermere, on the edges of the Leven Estuary and in the rockpools of Morecambe Bay. There's also an overview of marine life in the Lake District before tanks representing some of the water habitats of Asia, the Americas and Africa. Look out for the grinning caiman in the Tropical Rainforest and the Virtual Dive Bell. You can catch a boat from Bowness to Lakeside (p 12, ❶) and combine the aquarium visit with a steam train trip (❸). *Lakeside.* ☎ *015395 30153. www.lakes aquarium.com. Admission £8.75 adults; £5.75 children 3–15 years; free under 3 years; £7.25 seniors; £20–£34.45 family tickets. Open daily 9am–5pm (last admission 4pm).*

❸ ★★ **Lakeside & Haverthwaite Railway.** Some adults will want to go on the steam train

The Lakeside & Haverthwaite Railway is next to the aquarium.

from pretty Lakeside station to Newby Bridge and Haverthwaite, not just to entertain the children but because it is a nostalgia trip for them too. You can alight at Haverthwaite for refreshment at the small café or head straight back down the line where there's another café and shop. The ride is just long enough to keep kids happy. *Lakeside/Haverthwaite.* ☎ *015395 31594. www. lakesiderailway.co.uk. Admission £5.70 adult return; £3.45 adult single; £2.85 child return; £2.30 child single; £15.50 family. Open Apr–Oct first train from Haverthwaite daily 10.40am; last from Lakeside 4.50pm (3.45pm for last week of Oct).*

④ ★★★ **South Lakes Wild Animal Park.** Close to the south Cumbrian coast, this animal park provides a great family day out. There are some unusual and endangered creatures at the park, as well as more familiar ones like lions, bears and monkeys. The giraffes are always a great hit, stretching their necks over the fence to inspect the staring visitors, as are the rhinos, which sometimes breed here, and the penguins. To save your legs, you can take a miniature steam train

from one end of the park to the other. *Broughton Road, Dalton-in-Furness.* ☎ *01229 466086. www. wildanimalpark.co.uk. Admission £11.50 adults; £8 children 3–15 yrs and seniors; free under 3 yrs; £1.50 friends of the park. Open Easter–Nov daily 10am–5pm; Nov–Easter daily 10am–4.30pm. Train to Dalton-in-Furness; bus X9 from Bowness and Windermere.*

⑤ ★★★ **Muncaster Castle.** Muncaster is bliss for children, with a haunted castle and a huge estate, woodland, playgrounds and a maze. The World Owl Trust, in the castle grounds, is a sanctuary for various curious-looking breeds of owl, which are brought, blinking from their cages, during the daily shows (2.30pm). Towards the end of each afternoon, Muncaster's resident herons are fed. They gather in the trees in anticipation of their fishy dinner. When it's thrown to them, the subsequent commotion provides a good photo opportunity.

The MeadowVole Maze, a trail-based quiz through the grounds, is another popular activity for children. There are picnic areas, and Creeping Kate's Kitchen, where

Get a panoramic view of Whitehaven from The Beacon.

cakes and snacks are served most of the day.

For more information on the castle and gardens, see p 42, ③. *Muncaster, nr Ravenglass.* ☎ *01229 717614. www.muncaster.co.uk. Admission gardens, owl centre and maze £6 children 5–15 yrs; £26 family; free under 5 yrs. Open mid-Mar–beginning Nov gardens, maze and owl centre daily 10.30am–6pm; castle Sun–Fri 12pm–4.30pm. Train to Ravenglass station (circa 1 mile).*

⑥ ★★ **The Beacon.** Whitehaven's Beacon is an award-winning museum on the west Cumbrian coast, spread over several floors. From the top floor there are fabulous views of the Irish Sea, town and surrounding countryside, and telescopes which give you a closer look. The museum's fun and educational interactive exhibits explore Whitehaven's history, including Roman artifacts found in the area, the growth and decline of Whitehaven's harbour, its trade in rum, slaves and tobacco and the town's Georgian architecture, In fact, you'll see everything from armour to fine and decorative art. *West Strand.* ☎ *01946 592302. www.thebeacon-whitehaven.co.uk. Admission £5 adults; £4 concessions; under 16 yrs free with adult. Open Tues–Sun and bank holiday Mon 10am–4.30pm.*

⑦ ★★★ **Honister Slate Mine.** Older, braver kids will enjoy tackling the via ferrata, an ingenious introduction to climbing techniques (p 160, ⑤). There are also several age-graded mine tours for which you're given a hard hat. The Kimberly tour, open to all ages, is mostly on the flat and is a fully

At the South Lakes Animal Park, you can get a bird's-eye view of the animals from raised walkways.

guided introduction to mining at Honister. It's also the one recommended for rainy days. For The Edge tour you need to be over 1.3m tall, as it takes you to the edge of the mountain then upwards and deep inside, while The Cathedral ventures into the working mine and includes anecdotes from the mine's owner. *Honister Pass, Borrowdale.* ☎ *017687 77230 for information and mine tours;* ☎ *017687 77714 Via Ferrata tickets. www.honister-slate-mine.co.uk. Admission mine tours £9.75 adults; £4.75 under 16yrs; via ferrata £25–£35 adults; £20–£25 children; all-day pass (mine tour, lunch and via ferrata) £37–£48 adults; £28–£34 under 16yrs; £125–£160 family (2+2). Open daily 9am–5pm. Stagecoach Rambler 78.*

⑧ ★★ The Cumberland Pencil Museum. Armed with the quizzes they receive on arrival, children set off around this unusual small museum intent on tracking down the answers. The museum covers 350 years of the pencil-making industry in Keswick. A visit starts with an atmospheric wander through the replica Borrowdale mine where graphite was first discovered. After that, you learn everything there is to know about pencil-making, passing through the pencil registry with original pencil recipes and displays of vintage pencil packaging; the old machinery that produced the pencils and the longest pencil in the world are on display here. There are also some fascinating wartime 'spy pencils' containing tiny rolled-up maps of enemy territory and a video showing how pencils are made today. Afterwards, kids can hone any budding artistic skills with the multi-coloured crayons on sale in the shop. *Southey Works,* ☎ *017687 73626. www.pencilmuseum.co.uk.*

Kids can try practice their drawing skills at The Cumberland Pencil Museum.

Admission £3.25 adults; £1.75 under 16 yrs and seniors; £2.50 students. Open daily 9.30am–5pm.

⑨ ★★ Rheged. This ambitious family attraction combines shops, restaurants and activities with a touch of mystery and magic from bygone times. Spread over six floors, it is a discovery centre with giant movies of dinosaurs and other popular favourites, and exhibitions on Cumbria during the Ice Age. What is also appealing to kids is the Create workshop, where you choose a piece of pottery, paint it and take it home afterwards. There's a soft-play area for smaller children, and adventure playgrounds outside where older ones can run off surplus energy, with a Roman fort, Celtic round tower, turrets, tunnels and climbing walls. *Junction of A66 and A592.* ☎ *01768 868000. www.rheged.com. Admission giant movies £4.95 adults; £3.95 concessions; £3 children 5–15 yrs; £14 family (2 adults and 3 children); outdoor play £1.50 per child; indoor soft-play free–£2.50 per hour under 6mths–over 1 yr; Create £3.50–£6.95 per item.*

Kids can meet the cows at the Ice Cream Farm.

Take a Break

10 Abbott Lodge Jersey Ice Cream. Known to my nieces as the 'ice cream farm', this is the perfect kid's treat. Outside there's a play park with picnic benches and a chance to peek at the calves in the shed, while inside there's a soft-play area and the all-important ice cream and tea room. *Clifton, nr Penrith.* ☎ *01931 712720. Admission free—pay for ice cream! Open daily 11am–5pm.*

⑪ ★★★ Bird of Prey Centre.

Close to Lowther Castle, this centre offers close encounters with lots of fierce creatures, including eagles, hawks and falcons. Come during the daily flying display and you may get a chance to hold the birds, wearing a large protective glove. *Lowther, near Penrith,* ☎ *01931 712746. Admission £8 adults; £6 seniors and students; £4 children; free under 6yrs. Open daily 11am–5pm; flying displays daily 2pm–4pm.* ●

Eating with Kids

Almost all the attractions listed above have cafés, so you don't have to stray far for refreshment (and conveniences). These include: World of Beatrix Potter's The Tailor of Gloucester™ Tea Room, which has an outdoor terrace and baby-changing facilities; Rheged has three cafés that use fresh local ingredients and have kids' menus; South Lakes Wild Animal Park's Maki Restaurant has sandwiches, jacket potatoes and burgers, and both indoor and outdoor picnic areas if you've brought your own provisions. At Muncaster Castle there's a selection of hot and cold food and snacks at Creeping Kate's Kitchen, and there's a café at The Beacon with views over the harbour.

Central **Lake District**

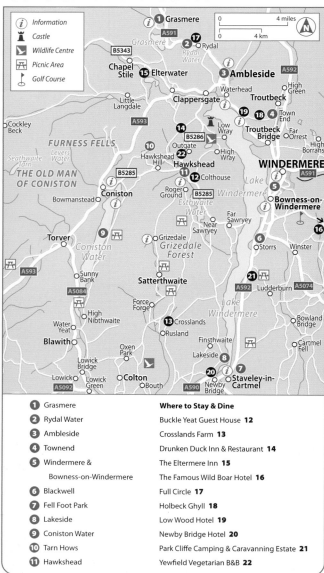

Legend:
- (i) Information
- Castle
- Wildlife Centre
- Picnic Area
- Golf Course

Map labels:

Grasmere
A591
Grasmere
B5343
Chapel Stile
15 Elterwater
2 17 Rydal
Rydal Water
3 Ambleside
A592
Waterhead
High Green
Little Langdale
Clappersgate
Troutbeck
19 18 Town End
A593
14
B5286
Low Wray
Cockley Beck
Seathwaite Tarn
Levers Water
FURNESS FELLS
10
Outgate
22
Hawkshead Hill
High Wray
Troutbeck Bridge
Far Orrest
High Borrans
THE OLD MAN OF CONISTON
B5285
Hawkshead
11 12 Colthouse
WINDERMERE
A591
Bowmanstead
(i) **Coniston**
(i)
Roger Ground
B5285
Esthwaite Water
5
Lake Windermere
Bowness-on-Windermere
Torver
9
Coniston Water
Near Sawrey
Far Sawrey
16
Sunny Bank
(i) Grizedale
Grizedale Forest
6 Storrs
Winster
A5084
Satterthwaite
21
Ludderburn
A5074
Force Forge
Lake Windermere
High Nibthwaite
13 Crosslands
Rusland
Finsthwaite
Bowland Bridge
Water Yeat
Cartmel Fell
Blawith
Oxen Park
Lakeside
8
Lowick Bridge
Colton
20
7
Lowick   Lowick Green
Bouth
Newby Bridge
Staveley-in-Cartmel
A5092
A590

Scale: 0 — 4 miles / 0 — 4 km

Windermere and Coniston Water, and the smaller lakes of Rydal Water and Grasmere, attract the lion's share of visitors to the Lake District. This tour is aimed at those who want to take in the best of the Central Lakes area over a few days. It doesn't stray too far off the beaten track, but takes in renowned attractions such as Beatrix Potter's Hill Top Farm and William Wordsworth's home at Rydal Mount and the popular villages of Grasmere and Hawkshead. In between the towns and villages, it suggests visits to Townend, Blackwell and Brantwood historic houses, and where to stop for a picnic. START: **Grasmere. A591 4–5 days.**

1 ★★★ Grasmere. This pretty village becomes very busy during peak season and holidays. To avoid the main crowds, arrive here first thing in the morning or towards the end of the day. Wordsworth fans make a pilgrimage to **St Oswald's Church** to see the Wordsworth graves, and to **Dove Cottage** and **The Wordsworth Museum and Art Gallery** (p 39, **5**). Grasmere is full of cafés and gift shops; many visitors make a beeline for the famous **Grasmere Gingerbread Shop.** Grasmere's scenic little lake is popular for leisurely strolls and boating, while the local fells of Great Rigg and Helm Crag offer more energetic hikes. *For more on Grasmere, see p 115.*

2 ★ Rydal Water. Just east of Grasmere on the busy A591, Rydal Water is only about half as big as its neighbour (about ¾ mile long), but just as entrancing. As at Grasmere, paths lead right round the shoreline. You can walk the entire way round one or both of the lakes, stopping on the Loughrigg Fell (south) side of Rydal Water to visit Rydal Cave, at the entrance to a former slate mine. Look out for Wordsworth's Seat, a rocky outcrop at the western end of the lake, reputedly a favourite spot of the poet (parking nearby).

3 ★★★ Ambleside. Continuing south-east along the A591, you reach this attractive town, a popular base for walkers and sightseers.

Grasmere has several gift shops, hotels and restaurants.

Wordsworth loved to stroll around Rydal Water.

You can stroll to take in the sight of water pouring down Stock Ghyll Force, particularly impressive after a downpour, and visit the remains of Ambleside Roman Fort, or pick up bargains in the outdoor shops that line its streets. There is a good selection of B&Bs and eateries, and several pubs serve real ales. *For more on Ambleside, see p 97.*

④ ★ **Townend.** Just off the A591 near Windermere, the village of Troutbeck has several carefully preserved 17th- and 18th-century houses, including Townend. This traditional stone-and-slate house once belonged to a wealthy yeoman family; today it's a National Trust property open to the public. You can wander through the kitchen and servants' quarters, where actors in period dress recreate the atmosphere of Townend's 17th-century heyday. Children can follow a discovery trail. *Troutbeck.* ☎ *015394 32628. www.nationaltrust.org.uk. Admission by guided tour only £4.40 adults; £2.20 children; £11 families. Open Mar weekends only 11am–3pm; Apr–Nov 11am–3pm. Drop-off point only—parking available 250 metres from the house.*

⑤ ★★★ **Windermere & Bowness-on-Windermere.** The town of Windermere merges seamlessly into lakeshore Bowness; if you're staying here, you can virtually roll out of bed on to a boat. It is undoubtedly one of the busiest and most popular parts of the Lake District, but if you don't mind crowds, there's plenty to do here (see Full-Day Tours p 12, ①). There are galleries and speciality shops selling crafts and hand-made chocolate, a host of watersports and lakeside walks, the **World of Beatrix Potter**

Bowness is a popular waterside leisure destination.

Boats on Windermere.

for younger children, and an excellent range of accommodation from B&B to luxury lakeside hotels. *For more on Bowness and Windermere, see p 102.*

6 ★★★ **Blackwell.** This **Arts & Crafts** building just off the Kendal Road is one of my favourite Lake District houses. Dazzlingly crafted naturalistic details and jewel colours embellish the structure inside and out. The dark wooden-panelled Main Hall contrasts with the pure White Drawing Room. *For more information on Blackwell, see p 45,* **7**. Bowness-on-Windermere, B5360 (just off the B5074). ☎ 015394 46139. www.blackwell.org.uk. Admission £6.95 adults; £4.10 children and students; £18.50 family. Open daily 10.30am–5pm (closes two weeks early Jan).

7 **Fell Foot Park.** On the southern shores of Lake Windermere, just off the A592, this National Trust park is a perfect picnic spot place. Enjoy a leisurely few hours admiring the lake views from the lawns, hire a rowing boat or, in summer, take ferries across to Lakeside (see **8**).

8 ★★ **Lakeside.** You can either drive to Lakeside or park at Haverthwaite and take a steam-train ride via Newby Bridge. The Lakes Aquarium is a family favourite, and there are lots of boat trips to Bowness and Ambleside. You can also hire bicycles from Country Lanes (p 157) and explore some of the routes through the Grizedale Forest Park (p 156).

Continue on the A590 to Haverthwaite, where you can join the South Lakes tour (p 91). Otherwise, turn right onto the A5092 (at the start of the dual carriageway when you see the Greenodd Estuary widening into Morecambe Bay on your left). Drive through Penny Bridge and right onto the A5084, heading north towards Coniston.

Blackwell is a fine example of an Arts & Crafts house.

Ferries travel across Windermere to Lakeside.

9 ★★★ **Coniston Water.** The southern end of Coniston Water is a good place to stop for a picnic and enjoy the lake views. There are a couple of parking places, including one by the water's edge with picnic tables. In summer, ferries operate from this point to Torver, about half way along the lake. Continue north on the A5084, heading away from the water to Torver, before turning right onto the A593 and heading to Coniston. This small town is home to the Ruskin Museum (p 110, **1**) which contains a valuable collection of Donald Campbell memorabilia (see below) and items connected with the art critic and social thinker John Ruskin, who lived at Brantwood on the opposite side of the lake (p 112). Also in Coniston are Ruskin's grave and a memorial to Campbell (p 67). Real ale fans might want to sample the brews at the Black Bull Inn, made in the microbrewery behind the pub.

From Coniston's waterfront jetty, you can take a boat trip across to Brantwood (p 112). The most interesting way to do this is to take a ride on the National Trust's restored steam yacht *Gondola*.

Keen walkers will head for the local fell known as the Old Man of Coniston (p 152). Less strenuous routes lead around the lakeshore. *For more on Coniston, see p 110.*

10 ★★★ **Tarn Hows.** William Wordsworth recommended visiting this idyllic stretch of water in his *Guide Through the District of the Lakes* (1835), Back then there were actually three smaller tarns, Low, Middle and High Tarn, but they merged into one when a dam was built. The lakeshore walk is wheelchair-accessible and easy enough for children to manage. There are plenty of benches around the lake where you can stop for a picnic and enjoy the picturesque views of tiny islets and distant fells. *For more beginners' walks, see p 149.*

11 ★★★ **Hawkshead.** Hawkshead is a pretty village with a few narrow winding streets, cafés and pubs. Notable places to visit include **Hawkshead Grammar School**, once attended by William Wordsworth, and the **Beatrix Potter Gallery** (p 120, **4**). A couple of miles outside of the village (along the B5285) is the popular Beatrix

Donald Campbell

Donald Campbell was born in 1921 in Surrey, inheriting a love of speed from his dare-devil father, Sir Malcolm Campbell, who held 13 world land and waterspeed records during the 1920s and 1930s.

Donald's attempts on the world water-speed record began in his father's Bluebird K4, but it was in the Bluebird K7 that he achieved an impressive total of seven successive world records between 1955 and 1964, the first claimed on Ullswater. He also achieved the world land-speed record in 1964. In 1967, he made his final doomed attempt on the world record in the modified Bluebird K7 on Coniston Water. At speeds exceeding 300mph, the boat suddenly reared out of the water, flipped over backwards and instantly disintegrated, plunging to the icy depths of the lake over 180 feet below. Campbell's body was eventually recovered, along with the remains of Bluebird K7, in 2001, and he was finally laid to rest on 12th September that year.

Potter house **Hill Top** (p 119, ➊). If you head south of Hawkshead past the Grammar School, you'll reach the **Grizedale Forest Park**, where you'll find woodland walks and mountain bike trails (p 156). For something more gentle, try trout fishing on Esthwaite Water. *For more on Hawkshead, see p 119.*

The southern end of Coniston Water is a peaceful place for a picnic.

Where to **Stay & Dine**

Buckle Yeat Guest House

NEAR SAWREY This traditional Lakeland cottage near Hill Top featured in Beatrix Potter's *Tale of Tom Kitten.* Unless it's raining, you'll see another of her characters outside, a life-size 'Mr McGregor' (made from chicken wire with clothes on), donated by a lady who made him for a scarecrow competition. Visitors have their photo taken with him in exchange for a few pennies, which are donated to children's charities. Inside there are several bedrooms and downstairs an oak-beamed lounge with a roaring log fire in winter. *Near Sawrey.* ☎ *015394 36446. www.buckle-yeat. co.uk. Doubles from £80. AE, Maestro, MC, V.*

Crosslands Farm

CONISTON A traditional 17th-century Lakeland farm between Coniston Water and Windermere and just minutes from Grizedale Forest and Hawkshead. The guestrooms are individually styled in neutral or pastel hues with valley or fell views. *Rusland.* ☎ *01229 860242. www.crosslands farm.co.uk. Doubles from £52; caravans £11.Cash or cheque only.*

Drunken Duck Inn & Restaurant

AMBLESIDE *BRITISH* Since 1977, this outstanding family-owned pub and restaurant with accommodation has gained many admirers. It's particularly famed for its gastropub fare and ales made in its own micro-brewery. There are stylish guestrooms above the pub or in a separate building to the rear, some with views of The Langdale Pikes. *Barn gates, Ambleside.* ☎ *015394 36347. www.drunkenduckinn.co.uk.*

Doubles £95–£275. Entrees lunch from £5.95, dinner from £13.95. AE, Maestro, MC, V.

The Eltermere Inn

AMBLESIDE The 15 recently refurbished rooms either have views of Elterwater or the Langdale Pikes. Downstairs is a beamed bar with a log fire and a traditional local menu of homemade soup, wild rabbit and Cumberland sausage and mash. *Elterwater, Ambleside.* ☎ *015394 37207. www. eltermere.co.uk. Doubles £100–£170. Menus £25, entrees from £8. Maestro, MC, V.*

The Famous Wild Boar Hotel

WINDERMERE *BRITISH* This former coaching inn in the Gilpin Valley has a pub-restaurant renowned for its real ales and seasonal local produce, such as shank of Lakeland lamb and haunch of wild boar. There's accommodation upstairs, some of which have four-poster beds with heavy drapes. *Crook, nr Windermere.* ☎ *015394 45225. www.elh.co.uk. Doubles £68–£196. Entrees from £8.50. AE, Maestro, MC, V.*

Full Circle

RYDAL WATER These luxury yurts (wooden-framed east Asian nomadic shelters, handmade in Mongolia) have a wood-burning stove and cooking equipment. There are also hot showers and a drinking water tap. Each yurt sleeps up to six, with a double bed, two singles and two roll mats. *Rydal Hall, Ambleside.* ☎ *07975 671928. www.lake-district-yurts.co.uk. Yurts Mon–Fri or Fri–Mon £265–£285, Fri–Fri, Mon–Mon £385–£440.Cheques, cash or bank transfer only.*

You need to book ahead for a table at the Drunken Duck Inn, near Hawkshead.

Holbeck Ghyll WINDERMERE
BRITISH A fine country-house hotel with views of Windermere from most rooms, this also has a Michelin-starred restaurant serving French and British cuisine. Lodge rooms have private balconies or patios. There's also a health spa. *Holbeck Lane, Windermere.* ☎ *015394 32375. www.holbeckghyll.com. Doubles from £210. Dinner menu from £55. AE, Maestro, MC, V.*

Low Wood Hotel WINDERMERE
EUROPEAN Set on the shores of Windermere, this large hotel has more than 100 guestrooms, a swimming pool, gym, marina and watersports centre (p 167). The Windermere Restaurant serves modern European cuisine, and there is a bistro menu in the Café del Lago. *Low Wood, Windermere.* ☎ *015394 33773. www.elh.co.uk. Doubles £96–£240.Entrees from £9.50. AE, Maestro, MC, V.*

Newby Bridge Hotel NEWBY
BRIDGE *BRITISH* This refurbished hotel has 41 classically styled rooms, some with four-poster beds, and family rooms leading onto the hotel courtyard. There's a gym,

indoor pool, steam room and spa, and a restaurant using seasonal produce from the hotel garden. *Newby Bridge.* ☎ *015395 31222. www.newbybridgehotel.co.uk. Doubles from £108. Menus from £22.50. AE, Maestro, MC, V.*

Park Cliffe Camping & Caravanning Estate NEWBY
BRIDGE At this well-equipped site, you have a choice of parking your motorhome, pitching a tent, renting a timber lodge or staying in a luxury caravan. You can even have a private bathroom if you want. On-site facilities include a restaurant, bar and a shop. *Birks Road, Newby Bridge.* ☎ *015394 31344. www.parkcliffe.co.uk. Tents and campers £9.50–£26.50. Maestro, MC, V.*

Yewfield Vegetarian B&B
HAWKSHEAD Refurbished with high-quality traditional furnishings, this B&B also has self-catering cottages. Breakfast includes a continental buffet or a cooked breakfast using locally sourced organic produce. *Hawkshead Hill.* ☎ *015394 36765. www.yewfield.co.uk. Doubles £70–£120. 1–2 bed s/c apartments £280–£550 per week. Maestro, MC, V.*

East Lakes

Information (i)

Castle

Wildlife Centre

Picnic Area

Golf Course

1 Kendal

2 Staveley Mill Yard

3 The Greyhound Hotel

4 Shap Abbey

5 Haweswater

6 Askham

7 Penrith

8 Dalemain House

9 Ullswater

10 Kirkstone Pass

Where to Stay & Dine

Crown & Mitre Inn **11**

Deepdale Hall **12**

The Eagle & Child Inn **13**

Helsington Laithes Manor **14**

Kirkstone Pass Inn **15**

Lowthwaite B&B **16**

Patterdale Hall Estate **17**

The Pooley Bridge Inn **18**

Punchbowl Inn & Restaurant **19**

Sharrow Bay **20**

Waterside House Campsite **21**

The East Lakes edge up to the M6 motorway, but this tour takes a more scenic route from Kendal to Shap village and market town Penrith. The route is influenced by my weekends spent exploring chocolate box villages such as Askham, cycling through the Lowther Estates to Penrith or over the hill to Pooley Bridge, on the banks of Ullswater. The Lake District's second-largest lake, it is a favourite for watersports, boat rides and visits to Aira Force, a cascading waterfall surrounded by woodland walks. The tour also visits Dalemain stately home and gardens and ends with spectacular Lakeland views from Kirkstone Pass, where you can see all the way to Windermere. START: **Kendal. A6 4–5 days. Transport: bus 552, 555, X1, 107; train to Kendal station.**

① ★★★ **Kendal.** You could easily spend a whole day here in Kendal, visiting celebrated attractions like The Quaker Tapestry, a modern take on Bayeux that tells the story of the Quakers from the 17th century to the present. Other museums include the Museum of Kendal Life, with reconstructed period rooms and *Swallows and Amazons* memorabilia; and nearby Abbott Hall, a grand Georgian house now used as an art gallery. It contains a collection of landscape paintings and hosts temporary modern art exhibitions. At Kendal Museum, you can go back further in time, discovering pre-history and the Romans. If you stay overnight in Kendal, you can enjoy some of the events staged at the Brewery Arts Centre. *For a full tour of Kendal, see p 123.*

② ★ **Staveley Mill Yard.** Just north of Kendal, Staveley is a gastronome's heaven, a former fulling mill (where sheep's wool was washed) that now houses several galleries and food and drink stores. You can get a good, basic feed at Wilf's Café, and take a tour of Hawkshead Brewery. Other businesses here include Windermere Ice Cream, Organico and Lucy Cooks School, where you can learn how to cook meat, gluten-free meals or join other specialist courses. *For more information on Staveley Mill Yard, see p 52,* **⑧**.

The Quaker Tapestry gives an insight into more than just needlework.

The Punchbowl in Askham is the perfect country pub.

Turning south on the A591 once again, you can take a short cut via Burneside through from the A591 to the A6, a beautiful winding route that leads to Shap.

Take a Break

3 **The Greyhound Hotel.** Just minutes from junction 39 of the M6, this traditional pub beats any motorway services hands down. Enjoy British favourites like steak and ale pie with a pint of regional ale. *Main Street, Shap.* ☎ *01931 716474. www.greyhoundshap.co.uk. Entrees £9–£14.50. AE, DC, MC, V. Lunch and dinner daily. Closed public hols.*

Shap Abbey was founded in the early 13th century.

4 ★ **Shap Abbey.** About a mile west of Shap's Main Street, this evocative ruin in a rural setting justifies the short detour. Shap Abbey was once home to a community of Premonstratensian canons (a Catholic religious order founded in 1120 at Premontré in France). A local baron granted the land to the canons in around 1200 and the abbey remained here until it was suppressed during the Reformation in the 16th century. Part of it was later used as a farm but most of the original abbey walls were knocked down so the building materials could be recycled elsewhere. The main portal and tower are still standing and you can see the outline of the church and other buildings. *Pow Lane, Shap.*

5 ★ **Haweswater.** Farther east (reached on a minor road via Bampton Grange), Haweswater is a reservoir (see below). Underneath it lie the former villages of Measand and Mardale Green, flooded when the reservoir was opened in 1935. A road runs south west along the wooded lakeshore from Burnbanks, with Bampton Common rising beyond. The road steadily climbs; mid-way, the Haweswater Hotel is a quiet getaway or the perfect place for afternoon tea overlooking the lake. The road ends abruptly at the end of the lake, but from here there are walking routes past Small Water and Blea Water tarns, and up to High Street (p 152, **17**), an ancient transport

Lowther Estates

Today the Lowther Estates extend from the outskirts of Penrith to Hackthorpe, encompassing farmland, houses, a holiday park and church. The centrepiece, however, is Lowther Castle, seat of the Lowther family.

The Lowthers can trace their history back to the 12th century, when they were first mentioned in land grant documents during the reign of Henry II. Successive generations of Lowthers were knighted or ennobled and the family's influence gradually spread all the way through Westmorland (now part of Cumbria) to White-haven on the coast. The present head/landowner/incumbent of the Lowther Estates is Hugh Clayton, 8th Earl of Lonsdale.

route the Romans used in the 2nd century.

6 ★ Askham. North of Haweswater and Bampton, Askham is a picturesque village. Uphill to the east is Lowther Castle, an abandoned 19th-century folly on the vast Lowther Estates (see box above). There are two pubs and a small shop in Askham; the Queens Head retains several of its 17th-century beams, and the 18th-century Punchbowl is popular with visitors for its food and cosy atmosphere (p 77). From Askham you can take a shortcut through to Ullswater (**9**) via Celleron, or walk up to High Street via Askham Fell (p 152, **17**).

7 ★ Penrith. Carry on via the A6 as far as Penrith. This busy market town has a number of interesting independent family-run shops, such as The Toffee Shop and Cranston's (a traditional, old-fashioned butchers (p 49, **2**). Local attractions nearby include Penrith Castle and

Underneath Haweswater reservoir lie the remains of two villages.

Glenridding is a popular starting point for climbing Helvellyn.

Broughton Castle and Rheged, a multi-activity discovery centre. *For a full tour of Penrith, see p 135.*

⑧ ★ Dalemain House. Take the A592 road south-west from the Rheged roundabout. The gates of Dalemain House appear shortly on the right-hand side. The façade is Georgian but the original house is much older. Built in medieval times as a fortified pele tower, additions followed through the centuries, including a 14th-century hall and

Brougham Castle was built on the site of a Roman fort.

second tower. It was enlarged considerably during the 16th century and finally the Georgian front was added in the 18th century. Inside, the house is a warren of passages and stairways. Rooms contain an impressive assembly of family portraits, antique furnishings and old toys. Stop for a cup of tea in the Medieval Hall Tearoom before exploring the gardens outside, which are best for bluebells in May, scented roses in July and clematis in late summer. *Dalemain.* ☎ *017684 86450. www.dalemain.com. Admission by guided tour only in mornings. House and gardens £8.50 adults; gardens only £6 adults; free up to 4 accompanied children house or garden. Open early Apr–end Oct Sun–Thurs 11.15am–4pm (3pm in Oct) tearooms, gardens and gift shop 10.30am–5pm; Nov–Feb gardens and tearooms only Sun–Thurs 11am–4pm.*

⑨ ★ Ullswater. Continue on the A592 from Dalemain along the shores of Ullswater to the car park at Waterfoot. Walk across the bridge to Pooley Bridge's cafés and gift shops and enjoy a waterfront stroll through the Park Foot campsite. Or take a boat from near the car park to

Withnail and I

Withnail and I (1986) is a Sixties-set film based in London's Camden Town and various locations near Shap in Cumbria. Written and directed by Bruce Robinson, the film follows two out-of-work actors, Withnail (Richard E Grant) and I (Paul McGann) from their squalid London flat to the country house of Withnail's eccentric, gay Uncle Monty. Both farcical and comic, the film became a cult classic, and since then fans have made the pilgrimage to various film locations, including those in Cumbria. After years of dispute over restrictive planning permission, the country house, Sleddale Hall (Crow Crag in the film) at Wet Sleddale Reservoir near Shap, was finally sold to a Withnail fan in 2009, to be used as a private home, so you'll need to be friends with the owner to be able to visit. Many come searching for The King Henry Pub and the Penrith Tea-rooms, which featured in the film, but the actual film location for these was Buckinghamshire. For more Withnail and I trivia, see www.withnail-links.com.

Howtown and Glenridding, a popular tourist destination and starting point for the hike up Helvellyn (p 151). If you continue driving along the A592, you can stop at the National Trust-run Aira Force and follow woodland walks around the waterfall.

⑩ ★ Kirkstone Pass. The A592 road continues through Glenridding and Patterdale, climbing uphill past Brothers Water and over the spectacular Kirkstone Pass (p 19, ⑧). There's an inn and a car park at the top, with views straight down to Lake Windermere. From here you can drive on to Ambleside or Windermere and join the Central Lakes tour.

There are spectacular views all the way to Windermere from Kirkstone Pass.

Where to **Stay & Dine**

The Punchbowl in Askham.

Crown & Mitre Inn HAWESWA-TER A recently refurbished country pub with contemporary guest-rooms, the Crown & Mitre is close to the Coast-to-Coast trail (p 152). The food includes dishes like steak and ale pie, pheasant breast and sea bass. *Main Street, Bampton Grange.* ☎ *01931 713225. www. crown-and-mitre.co.uk. Doubles £70–£80. Entrees from £9.95. Maestro, MC, V.*

Deepdale Hall ULLSWATER A Grade II-listed 17th-century farm-house, this B&B is located on a working farm near Ullswater. The comfortable country-style rooms have views towards High Street, and there is also a cottage to rent on-site with two bedrooms. *Patterdale.* ☎ *017684 82369. www.deepdale hall.co.uk. Doubles from £80. Maestro, MC, V.*

The Eagle & Child Inn STAVE-LEY At the heart of foodie village Staveley, this inn has comfy country B&B accommodation. The bar places an emphasis on real ale and serves hearty dishes like Hawkshead ale pie, lamb shank and veggie lasagne.

Kendal Road, Staveley. ☎ *01539 821320. www.eaglechildinn.co.uk. Doubles £65–£95. Entrees £9.95. AE, Maestro, MC, V.*

Helsington Laithes Manor KENDAL This property dates back to the 15th century and guestrooms are furnished with antiques. There are some adjoining rooms and twins available. *Helsington, Kendal.* ☎ *01539 741253. www.helsington. co.uk. Doubles from £70. Maestro, MC, V.*

Kirkstone Pass Inn KIRKSTONE PASS Cumbria's highest inn, this pub has a spectacular position at the highest point of Kirkstone Pass. It serves locally sourced beer and food, including Kirkstone Porter. Comfortable guestrooms and a bunkhouse mean you don't have far to stumble. *Kirkstone Pass.* ☎ *015394 33888. www.kirkstone passinn.com. Doubles from £65. Bunk house from £8.50pp. Cash only.*

Lowthwaite B&B ULLSWATER This recently refurbished old farm-house lies west of Ullswater. There are four comfortable rooms and the food is locally sourced, organic or fair-trade. Evening meals are available. *Patterdale.* ☎ *017684 82343. www.lowthwaiteullswater.com. Doubles from £70. Maestro, MC, V.*

Patterdale Hall Estate

ULLSWATER At the southern end of Ullswater, this estate has a choice of wooden chalets, stone cottages and bothies. All have fully equipped kitchens. *Patterdale.* ☎ *017684 82308. www.phel.co.uk. Accommodation £178–£491 per week. Maestro, MC, V.*

The Pooley Bridge Inn

ULLSWATER *BRITISH* This hotel is something of a landmark in Pooley Bridge, with its distinctive black balcony. The guestrooms are traditional, some with four-poster beds, others suitable for families. Downstairs, there's a bare-stone bar with an open fire and a restaurant serving British pub favourites. *Pooley Bridge.* ☎ *017684 86215. www. pooleybridgeinn.co.uk. Doubles £75–£110. AE, Maestro, MC, V.*

Punchbowl Inn & Restaurant

ASKHAM This pretty village pub has six contemporary guestrooms. In winter, there's a roaring fire in the bar-restaurant, and seating outside in the summer. Choose from its range of dishes from traditional fish pie to Moroccan vegetable tagine. *Askham.* ☎ *01931 712443. www. punchbowlaskham.co.uk. Doubles from £85. Entrees from £10. Maestro, MC, V.*

Sharrow Bay ULLSWATER This Ullswater hotel has been renowned as a country retreat for more than half a century. People come for its lakeside setting and Michelin-starred restaurant specializing in fine British cuisine. The guestrooms are classically dressed in elaborate textiles and antiques. *Ullswater, Penrith.* ☎ *01768 486301. www. sharrowbay.co.uk. Doubles £200–£700. Lunch menu from £43. Dinner menu from £70. AE. Maestro, MC, V.*

Waterside House Campsite

ULLSWATER A family-run campsite in a splendid setting on the northern shores of Ullswater. There's an on-site shop. *Howtown Road, Pooley Bridge.* ☎ *017684 86332. www. watersidefarm-campsite.com. 2 adults, tent and car or motorhome £12–£22; extra person £3–£5.50. No caravans. Cash only.*

Waterside House Campsite is set on the banks of Ullwater.

North Lakes

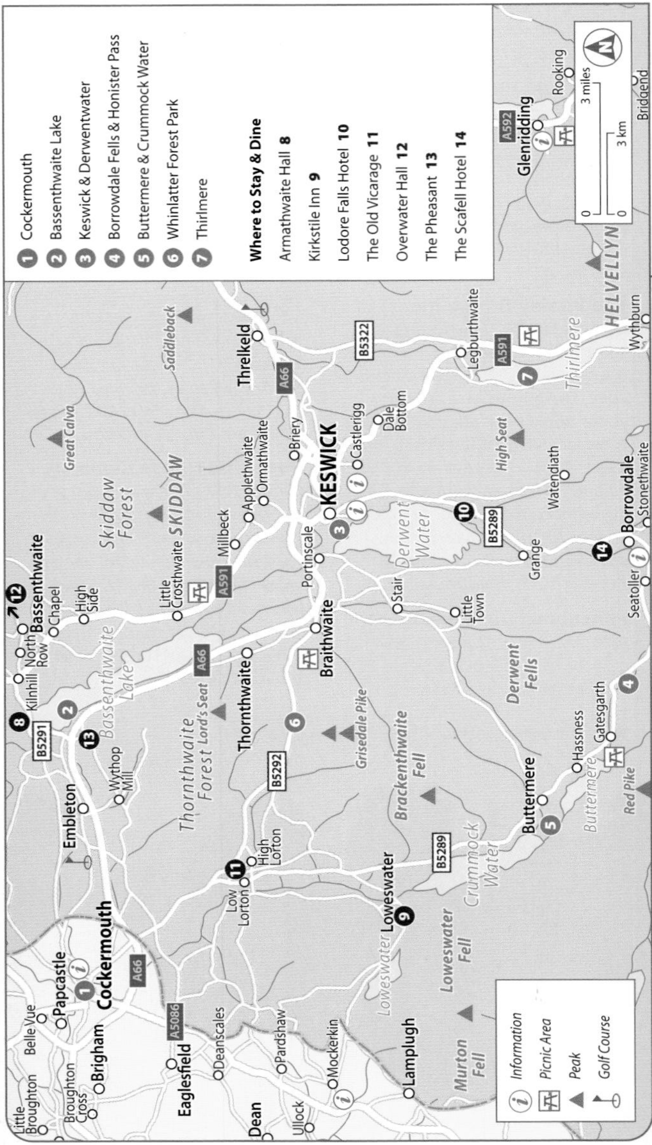
1 Cockermouth
2 Bassenthwaite Lake
3 Keswick & Derwentwater
4 Borrowdale Fells & Honister Pass
5 Buttermere & Crummock Water
6 Whinlatter Forest Park
7 Thirlmere
Where to Stay & Dine
Armathwaite Hall 8
Kirkstile Inn 9
Lodore Falls Hotel 10
The Old Vicarage 11
Overwater Hall 12
The Pheasant 13
The Scafell Hotel 14
Information
Picnic Area
Peak
Golf Course
0 3 miles
0 3 km
N
Little Broughton
Broughton Cross
Brigham
Belle Vue
Papcastle
Cockermouth
Eaglesfield
Dean
Deanscales
Pardshaw
Ullock
Mockerkin
Lamplugh
Murton Fell
Loweswater Fell
Loweswater
Low Lorton
High Lorton
Embleton
Wythop Mill
Kilnhill
North Row
Bassenthwaite
Chapel
High Side
Bassenthwaite Lake
Thornthwaite Forest
Lord's Seat
Thornthwaite
Braithwaite
Grisedale Pike
Brackenthwaite Fell
Crummock Water
Buttermere
Hassness
Gatesgarth
Red Pike
Derwent Fells
Little Crosthwaite
Millbeck
Skiddaw Forest
SKIDDAW
Great Calva
Saddleback
Applethwaite
Ormathwaite
Briery
Portinscale
KESWICK
Castlerigg
Dale Bottom
Threlkeld
Legburthwaite
Derwent Water
Stair
Little Town
Grange
Watendlath
High Seat
Borrowdale
Stonethwaite
Seatoller
Thirlmere
Wythburn
HELVELLYN
Glenridding
Rooking
Bridgend
A66
A5086
A591
A592
B5291
B5292
B5289
B5322

This tour takes in one of the most dramatic vistas in the Lake District, the Borrowdale Fells. As you pass the end of Derwentwater, the route winds upwards until you realize you've left the last Lakeland village below and can see nothing but hills sweeping down to the green of Honister Pass below. I found myself hundreds of feet up facing a rock face at Honister Slate Mine, knuckles white with gripping on. You can also appreciate the countryside at a gentler pace, mirrored in Buttermere's glass-like water or under the green canopy of Whinlatter Forest. Also on the tour are Georgian Cockermouth and Victorian Keswick, two contrasting towns with museums appealing to children, beer lovers and James Bond fans.

START: **Cockermouth. A66/A595. 3–5 days.**

1 ★★ Cockermouth. This Georgian town lies west of Bassenthwaite Lake, just outside the northern border of the Lake District National Park. One of its main sights is William Wordsworth's birthplace on Main Street, open to the public (National Trust) (see p 114). Another popular attraction for many visitors here is Jennings Brewery, which offers tours and tastings. *For a full tour of Cockermouth, see p 107.*

Exit Cockermouth via the Lamplugh Road and turn left onto the A66.

2 ★★ Bassenthwaite Lake. The region's only body of water with 'lake' officially in its title, Bassenthwaite is a quiet, sedate lake with a few hidden places to explore. The A591 leads along the east side of the lake, passing pretty Bassenthwaite village and Skiddaw, one of the Lake District's highest peaks, which looms behind it. Farther along the road is Mirehouse, a large stately home with a notable tearoom (p 41, **1**) and Dodd Wood, where there's an osprey viewing point. The A66 travels along the west side of the lake, past its mostly coniferous woodland.

3 ★★★ Keswick & Derwentwater. With a glorious lakeside

Jennings Brewery is a main attraction in Cockermouth.

Bassenthwaite Lake is within easy reach of Skiddaw and Blencathra.

location, a fine choice of fell walks and several wet-weather attractions, it's not surprising Keswick is so popular. In town, car and film fans head to Cars of the Stars and the recently opened James Bond Museum. The Cumberland Pencil Museum traces the history of a local industry, with activities for all the family, while the Keswick Museum includes an eclectic collection of curios such as the skin of a giant cobra and Britain's rarest fish, as well as letters from the Lakeland poets and Napoleon's teacup.

Derwentwater is surrounded by fells.

There's gentle cycling along the old railway tracks to Threlkeld (p 155), hop-on, hop-off boat rides around Derwentwater and a small hike up Catbells, a manageable climb for most reasonably fit visitors. If you're looking for more of a challenge, head for the fells of Skiddaw and Blencathra (p 152). *For a full tour of Keswick, see p 129.*

④ ★★★ **Borrowdale Fells & Honister Pass.** The B5289 runs south from Keswick along the length of Derwentwater and the River Derwent through woodland, before the road rises; before long you're surrounded by the dramatic scenery of the Borrowdale Fells to the left and the Derwent Fells to the right, with rocky peaks and steep green and sometimes wooded slopes. If you turn left at Seatoller, you'll come to the Seathwaite car park, a popular starting route for the hike up Great Gable (p 152), one of the Lake District's highest mountains. Alternatively, continue along the B5289 to Honister Slate Mine (p 160). You can spend a few hours or an entire day here touring the mines, traversing rock faces or buying slate crafts from the shop. Whichever you choose, the view down the valley to Honister Pass is worth stopping for,

The drive through Honister Pass offers spectacular scenery.

with Buttermere Fell rising sharply to the right.

5 ★★★ Buttermere & Crummock Water. The road descends along Honister Pass to Gatesgarth, a little car park just before Buttermere. There's another car park at Buttermere village, between Buttermere and Crummock Water, but you'll need to get here early in the day to find a space in high season. A traffic-free path runs most of the way around Buttermere; be wary of oncoming traffic on the short distance when you do have to walk on the road. The east side of Crummock Water involves more road-walking, but if you follow the path along the west bank, you can walk up to Scale Force, the highest waterfall in the Lake District. Several excellent hill walks start from these two lakes, including Hay Stacks, High Crag, High Stile, Red Pike and Dodd.

6 ★★ Whinlatter Forest Park. Back on the B5289, turn right at Low Lorton onto the B5292. The scenery quickly changes as you drive through Whinlatter Pass; before long you're surrounded by dense forest. Stop at the Whinlatter Visitor Centre for mountain biking and walking along forest trails, and the Go Ape high wire adventure.

Continue through the forest road until Braithwaite and head back into Keswick along the A66, turning right on the A591 towards Ambleside.

7 ★★ Thirlmere. Like Haweswater, Thirlmere is a reservoir lake, but much more easily accessible. The busy A591 runs down its eastern shore but you can drive around the quieter western shore stopping at roadside parking places to follow forest trails. Off the A591, Highpark Wood is the popular starting point for one of the main routes up Helvellyn, England's third-highest mountain (p 151).

Honister Slate Mine offers tours and a taste of climbing.

Where to **Stay & Dine**

Armathwaite Hall BASSENTH-
WAITE *MODERN BRITISH* Close to
Bassenthwaite Lake, Armathwaite
Hall is set within a deer park and
woodland. Accommodation ranges
from peaceful club rooms to luxury
studio suites with lake views. There
are several public spaces to read,
relax and enjoy drinks, a spa with a
pool and an ambitious restaurant
serving Cumbrian specialities. *Bassenthwaite Lake.* ☎ *017687 76551.
www.armathwaite-hall.co.uk. Doubles £240–£370. Menu lunch £23.95,
dinner £43.95. AE, Maestro, MC, V.*

Kirkstile Inn CRUMMOCK WATER
BRITISH A 400-year-old pub with
accommodation, the Kirkstile Inn is
tucked into a rural nook between
Crummock Water and Loweswater.
Stay in its country-style rooms and
dine on hearty plates of chicken,
leek and mustard pudding, washed
down with ales from their own
micro-brewery. *Loweswater.*
☎ *01900 85219. www.kirkstile.com.
Doubles from £87. Entrees from
£8.25. Maestro, MC, V.*

Lodore Falls Hotel DERWENT-
WATER This hotel has an enviable
position on the banks of Derwentwater, with a waterfall backdrop.
The traditional-style rooms have fell
or lake views, while the restaurant
enjoys views of both. After a day of

walking you can wind down in the
spa and beauty salon and enjoy evening drinks in the bar. *Borrowdale.*
☎ *017687 77285. www.lakedistrict
hotels.com. Doubles £150–£368.
Menu £33. AE, Maestro, MC, V.*

The Old Vicarage LORTON
Between Cockermouth and Whinlatter Forest, this B&B has a country
feel with cosy patchwork quilts and
bedspreads. Guests can order a
packed lunch for days out and enjoy
a two- or three-course dinner at
night. *Church Lane, Lorton.*
☎ *01900 85656. www.oldvicarage.
co.uk. Doubles £110–£160. Menu
£21–£25. AE, Maestro, MC, V.*

Overwater Hall BASSENTHWAITE
MODERN BRITISH This 18th-century
country house hotel, just north of
Bassenthwaite Lake, was opened by
Stephen Bore and Angela and Adrian
Hyde in 1992. Since then, they have
created a magnificent hotel with 11
bedrooms, each individually decorated to a high standard. Book a
table for dinner, and peruse the
menu beforehand with an aperitif in
the lounge. Chef-owner Adrian creates a daily changing menu that can
include mouth-watering dishes like
fillets of smoked seabass on a par-
mesan-cheese biscuit, or maple-
syrup glazed wild mallard with sherry
braised puy lentils. Guests often

Lakeland Camping Barns

Camping barns are the budget choice for serious walkers and
outdoor enthusiasts. Barns can vary but generally have cooking
facilities and cold water. Bring your own roll-mat and sleeping bag.
Borrowdale, Cockermouth, Kendal, Keswick, St Bees and Wasdale. ☎ *01946
758198. www.lakelandcampingbarns.com. Bed spaces £7 per person, per
night.*

Self-catering

There are literally hundreds of privately rented cottages throughout the Lake District. They range from traditional Lakeland cottages to converted barns, large modern houses to wooden chalets. For recommended accommodation, see Cumbria Tourism's website www.golakes.co.uk.

retire to the hallway sofas for coffee and chocolates. Dogs are permitted. *Ireby.* ☎ *017687 76566. www. overwaterhall.co.uk. Doubles £120–£210. Menu £40. Maestro, MC, V.*

The Pheasant BASSENTHWAITE *BRITISH* This former coaching inn close to Bassenthwaite Lake has a well-deserved reputation for its restaurant. For dinner there's a choice of three or four courses and main courses like sustainable cod with samphire, saffron potatoes and caviar butter sauce. You can stay here too, with a choice of comfortable standard rooms, garden rooms in a separate lodge and superior rooms with extra seating areas. *Bassenthwaite Lake Cockermouth.* ☎ *017687 76234. www.the-pheasant.co.uk. Doubles £146–£190. Menus lunch*

£22.50–£27.90, dinner £33.25–£37. Maestro, MC, V.

The Scafell Hotel BORROWDALE A renowned coaching inn, this hotel has a traditional bar and restaurant serving sandwiches, soup or hot lunches like Cumbrian game casserole. The table d'hote dinner menu includes classic favourites like smoked salmon and spaghetti bolognese along with rarer choices like griddled ostrich steak. The guestrooms have been refreshed with fashionable wallpaper and textiles to give a modern feel. *Rosthwaite, Borrowdale Valley.* ☎ *017687 77208. www.scafell. co.uk. Doubles £76–£169. Bar entrees £7; restaurant entrees £14.95; menu £28.50. Maestro, MC, V.*

Overwater Hall is a fabulous country retreat.

Western Lakes &
Cumbrian Coast

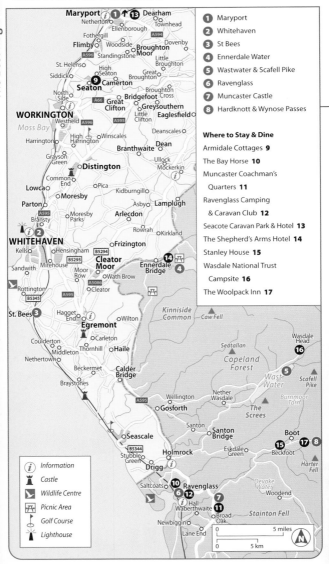

1. Maryport
2. Whitehaven
3. St Bees
4. Ennerdale Water
5. Wastwater & Scafell Pike
6. Ravenglass
7. Muncaster Castle
8. Hardknott & Wynose Passes

Where to Stay & Dine

Armidale Cottages **9**

The Bay Horse **10**

Muncaster Coachman's
Quarters **11**

Ravenglass Camping
& Caravan Club **12**

Seacote Caravan Park & Hotel **13**

The Shepherd's Arms Hotel **14**

Stanley House **15**

Wasdale National Trust
Campsite **16**

The Woolpack Inn **17**

i Information
🏰 Castle
Wildlife Centre
Picnic Area
Golf Course
Lighthouse

At the western extremity of the Lake District lie Scafell Pike, England's highest mountain; Ennerdale Water, the region's quietest lake; and a sweeping coastal road that edges up to the Irish Sea. This tour takes in it all, but you don't have to get active to appreciate the landscape and the area's attractions. You can marvel at the reflection of The Screes in Wastwater from the water's edge, or experience the drama of driving across Hardknott Pass. In Maryport and Whitehaven are museums exploring their maritime history and ancient Roman heritage, and Muncaster Castle introduces you to Tom Fool, a curious character from the past.

START: **Maryport. Transport: train to Maryport station.**

❶ ★★ **Maryport.** The **Senhouse Roman Museum** is one of Maryport's main attractions and comprises a collection of inscribed stones from a Roman fort and town that lay on the ridge next to the museum site. The collection, which was begun by John Senhouse in 1570, was rescued from the derelict family home in the 1960s and eventually placed in the current museum. Other attractions in Maryport include the **Lake District Coast Aquarium,** where you can see local marine and freshwater life, and **The Wave,** an entertainment and heritage centre near the harbour. There's also a small **Maritime Museum** telling the story of Maryport's seafaring past.

❷ ★ **Whitehaven.** South along the A595, Whitehaven retains several handsome Georgian town houses. Looking onto the renovated harbour, **The Beacon** is a hands-on museum of local history and culture especially popular with school parties. **The Rum Story** explores the rum and slave trades, and **The Haig Colliery Museum** the town's mining history. *For a full tour of Whitehaven, see p 144.*

The Solway Firth from Maryport.

The Beacon in Whitehaven is a hands-on look at the town's history.

3 ★ **St Bees.** The official starting point of Wainwright's long-distance Coast to Coast Walk (p 152), St Bees is also the most westerly point in Cumbria. The beach is best at low tide, when you can paddle in soft, smooth sand. Follow **the cliff-top path** (part of the Cumbria Coastal Way, p 153) to St Bees Lighthouse.

It's not manned today but the views from the top of St Bees Head are impressive.

4 ★ **Ennerdale Water.** The most remote and westerly of the lakes, Ennerdale lies inland from Whitehaven. The only road access is at the western end, near Ennerdale Bridge, but a network of cycle tracks and footpaths lead around it. From the eastern end, a hiking route heads towards Great Gable, but it's a long trek (see p 152).

5 ★ **Wastwater & Scafell Pike.** As you drive along Wastwater's western shore, The Screes loom over its western side reflected in the dark and brooding surface of England's deepest lake. The northern end of the lake is the main starting point for climbing Scafell Pike, England's highest mountain (see p 151), but it is the view towards Great Gable that has been immortalized in the Lake District National Park's logo since 2004. As well as well-trodden tracks up the mountains, you can follow footpaths around the lake or drive back south through the Copeland and Miterdale Forests.

Take in the views of Wastwater on the long climb up Scafell Pike.

Remains of a Roman boathouse at Ravenglass.

6 ★ **Ravenglass.** This small village lies at the mouth of three rivers, the Esk, Mite and Irk. The Romans took advantage of this strategic setting, building a naval base, Glannoventa, here in the 2nd century. Today all that remains is the bath house. There's a grassy bank beside the estuary, where you can enjoy a picnic and watch the trains come and go across the bridge. You can take coastal trains from here along the coast to St Bees, Whitehaven and Maryport. Kids and adults love the Ravenglass and Eskdale Railway, a seven-mile steamtrain line that travels along a beautiful route into the nearby rugged hills (see p 56).

7 ★ **Muncaster Castle.** The extensive grounds of this impressive castle look across the Eskdale Valley. Discover the history of the resident Pennington family, and find out about Tom Fool (p 26), and the World Owl Trust. *For more information, see p 42,* **3** *and p 57,* **5**. *Muncaster, nr Ravenglass.* ☎ *01229 717614. www.muncaster.co.uk. Admission gardens, owl centre and maze £8 adults; £6 children 5–15 yrs; free under 5 yrs. Castle upgrade £x +£2.50 adults; +£1 children; +£4 family. Open mid-Mar–beginning Nov gardens, maze and owl centre daily 10.30am–6pm; castle Sun–Fri 12pm–4.30pm. Train to Ravenglass station (around 1 mile).*

8 ★ **Hardknott & Wynose Passes.** This is one of the most spectacular drives anywhere in Britain—it's well worth braving the arduous hairpin bends for the amazing views, which are truly unforgettable on a clear autumn day when the sun is low in the sky. In high season this route can be exceptionally busy, and you may well need to pull over into passing points, not an easy feat on a bend at 45 degrees. Make sure your car is fit for the journey, as you'll spend most of the time in 2nd gear (or even 1st). Remember to fill up with fuel beforehand. (Strategies, p 8).

Where to **Stay & Dine**

Armidale Cottages MARYPORT
These pretty cottages offer B&B in
modern country-style rooms
between Maryport and Workington
on the Coast-to-Coast cycle route
(p 152). *29 High Seaton, Workington.*
☎ *01900 63704. www.armidale
cottages.co.uk. Doubles £65. Maestro, MC, V.*

The Bay Horse RAVENGLASS This
B&B is a former coaching inn with
sea views; guestrooms are in the
former stables. *Main Street, Ravenglass.* ☎ *01229 717015. www.bay
horseravenglass.com. Doubles £55–
£65. Cash or cheque only.*

**Muncaster Coachman's Quar-
ters** MUNCASTER Whether you're
on a ghost-hunting trip or just want
to enjoy the experience of staying
on this magnificent estate, these
converted outbuildings provide a
memorable stay. There's a fully
equipped kitchen within the building. *Muncaster Castle, Muncaster.*
☎ *01229 717614, www.muncaster.
co.uk. Doubles £75. Maestro, MC, V.*

**Ravenglass Camping & Cara-
van Club** RAVENGLASS Tucked
away on the western fringes of the
National Park, this tree-lined site is
perfect for families. Ravenglass village and the beach are within walking distance and trails lead from
here to Muncaster Castle. There are
on-site laundry facilities and a shop.
Ravenglass. ☎ *01229 717250.
www.siteseeker.co.uk. Adults £7.
10–£8.17; children £2.45–£2.54;
members' family deal £19.38–
£20.21; non-member pitches £6.46.
Maestro, MC, V.*

Seacote Caravan Park & Hotel
ST BEES This site is well placed for
walking the Coast-to-Coast route,
but is just as enjoyable as a seaside
base for exploring the western
Lakes. You can rent a static caravan,
bring your own tourer and tent or
book into the Seacote Hotel, with
spacious sea-view rooms and bar
and restaurant. *Beach Road, St
Bees. Caravan Park* ☎ *01946
822777, Hotel* ☎ *01946 822300.*

Ravenglass Camping and Caravan Club is great for families.

Wasdale Head, where you can stay at a National Trust campsite.

www.seacote.com. Static caravans £117–£416 per week; tourers/ motorhomes £18; tents £10–£18. Hotel doubles from £55. Maestro, MC, V.

The Shepherd's Arms Hotel

ENNERDALE This coaching inn is one of the nearest places to stay at Ennerdale Water, offering country-style guestrooms, Cumbrian ales and home-cooked pub grub. *Ennerdale Bridge.* ☎ *01946 861249. www.shepherdsarmshotel.co.uk. Doubles from £79. Maestro, MC, V.*

Stanley House

ESKDALE This B&B in the beautiful Eskdale Valley near the Ravenglass steam railway has tasteful modern guestrooms. Breakfast is served overlooking the picturesque gardens. *Eskdale.* ☎ *01946 723327. www.stanleyghyll-eskdale. co.uk. Doubles £80. AE, Maestro, MC, V.*

Wasdale National Trust Campsite

WASDALE Get close to nature at this campsite beside Wast-water at the foot of Scafell Pike. You can rent camping pods or take your own tent or caravan. *Wasdale Head, Wastwater.* ☎ *01946 726220. www. nationaltrust.org.uk. Pod £40; motorhomes and 1 adult £10.50; adult £4.50; child £2; tent £4–£8. Maestro, MC, V.*

The Woolpack Inn

HARDKNOTT In the Eskdale Valley just a couple of miles before Hardknott Roman Fort, this B&B inn has eight cosy rooms, six en suite. The restaurant serves hot and cold lunches and hearty pub dinners. There's also a micro-brewery so you can sup a few pints of Woolpacker and other Cumbrian ales. *Holmbrook, Copeland.* ☎ *019467 23230. www.woolpack. co.uk. Doubles £65–£120. Entrees from £11.50. Maestro, MC, V.*

South Lakes

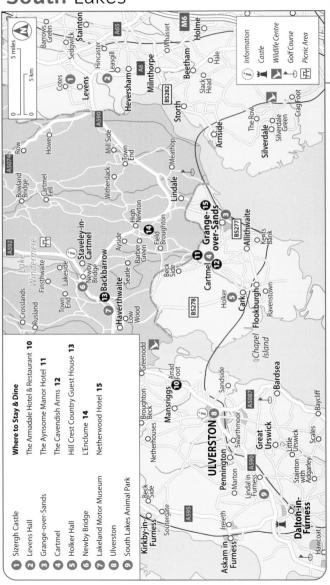

Where to Stay & Dine

The Armadale Hotel & Restaurant **10**

The Aynsome Manor Hotel **11**

The Cavendish Arms **12**

Hill Crest Country Guest House **13**

L'Enclume **14**

Netherwood Hotel **15**

1 Sizergh Castle

2 Levens Hall

3 Grange-over-Sands

4 Cartmel

5 Holker Hall

6 Newby Bridge

7 Haverthwaite

8 Ulverston

9 South Lakes Animal Park

Some of this South Lakes tour falls just outside the Lake District National Park, but it travels along a pretty route that leads into its heart. It takes in some important stately homes and gardens, including Sizergh Castle and Holker Hall, visits coastal Grange-over-Sands and Ulverston, birthplace of comic genius Stan Laurel, and ends with the South Lakes Animal Park. START: **Sizergh Castle. Transport: bus 552, 555.**

❶ ★★ Sizergh Castle. A short drive from Kendal, Sizergh Castle has been lived in continuously by the Strickland family since the Middle Ages. Today it is managed by the National Trust, although the family still occupies part of the property. The family portraits that adorn the walls here include works of the 17th–19th century English-school works as well as Italian and French sculpture. The exceptional wood-panelling of the Inlaid Chamber was returned here from London's Victoria & Albert Museum in 1999, while more recent renovations revealed the natural stone architecture of the building.

Outside, in the tranquil gardens, you can sit in the rock garden, stroll round the lawns that spread out in front of the castle and take in the views of Morecambe Bay. You can drive underneath the road from the castle grounds to Low Sizergh barn, a farm shop and café with regional produce (p 53, ❾). *Sizergh, nr Kendal* ☎ *015395 60951. www.national trust.org.uk. Admission £7.50 adults; £3.80 children; £18.80 family; garden only £4.90 adults; £2.50 children. Open mid-Mar–Oct castle Sun–Thurs 12pm–5pm; garden 11am–5pm. Bus 552, 555.*

❷ ★ Levens Hall. This mansion house stands on the opposite side of the A590. The original medieval pele tower was greatly expanded during Elizabethan times; its magnificent topiary gardens were added in the 17th century. Explore the history of the house and tuck into some local produce at the Bellingham Buttery

café. *For more information on Levens Hall, see p 46, ❾. Levens Hall (off A6/A590)* ☎ *015395 60321. www. levenshall.mullindesign.com. Admission house and gardens £10.50 adults; £4.50 children; £26 families; garden only £7.50 adults; £3.50 children; £19.50 family. Open early Apr–early Oct Sun–Thurs house 12pm–4.30pm; gardens and gift shop 10am–5pm. Bus 552, 555.*

❸ ★ Grange-over-Sands. This classic Edwardian seaside town overlooks Morecambe Bay. It's not ideal for swimming as the sea is located beyond a patch of marshland, but it's still a relaxing place and popular with older clientele who enjoy its sedate pace, strolls along its traffic-free promenade and the flowers in the ornamental gardens.

❹ ★ Cartmel. Turn right along Cartmel Road at Grange-over-Sands for Cartmel. Here you can visit the

Sizergh Castle dates back to the Middle Ages.

Cartmel Priory was closed during the Reformation.

12th-century Cartmel Priory, a medieval landmark that dominates this small village. The chancel is one of the oldest parts of the priory, where you can see medieval stained-glass windows. Another notable feature are the choir stalls, with 15th-century misericords (carvings which depict a range of grotesque faces) and intricate stall backs added in the 17th century. Outside, the village comprises a small collection of shops, pubs and restaurants. Pick up some sticky toffee pudding at Cartmel Village Store and maybe

treat yourself to a meal at Michelin-starred L'Enclume (p 94). Cartmel Racecourse is nearby (p 141).

⑤ ★ Holker Hall. Holker Hall in the village of Cark dates to the 16th century, but what remains of the original building is occupied by Lord and Lady Cavendish, whose family has lived here for over 400 years. The wing open to the public is a grand 19th-century building with valuable antiques, a library with over 3500 books and several bedrooms leading off The Gallery, a first-floor room popularized by the Elizabethans as the social hub of the house. *Cark-in-Cartmell.* ☎ *01539 558328. www.holker-hall.org.uk. Admission hall and gardens £10 adults; £9 seniors and students; £5.50 children 6–15 yrs; £27.50 family; garden only £6.50 adults; £5.50 seniors and students; £3.50 children 6–15 years; £16.50 family. Open hall mid-Mar–Oct Sun–Fri 11am–4pm; gardens Sun–Fri 10.30am–5.30pm; gift shop, restaurant and food hall. Feb–24 Dec daily 10.30am–5.30pm (4pm low season; 12pm on 24 Dec).*

⑥ ★ Newby Bridge. From here you can catch the Lakeside and Haverthwaite steam train. At

Stop in Ulverston to visit the Laurel and Hardy Museum.

The formal gardens at Holker Hall.

Lakeside you can visit the Lakeside Aquarium, take a boat across to Fell Foot Park for a picnic or a longer cruise to Bowness and Ambleside—see Central Lakes tour, ③–⑥, p 63.

⑦ ★ Lakeland Motor Museum.
By spring 2010 this museum will have moved from its former home at Holker Hall and re-opened in its new purpose-built home at Backbarrow, between Haverthwaite and Newby Bridge, where it will have more space and be able to reorganize its 30,000 or so exhibits. Whether you're a motoring enthusiast or just enjoy a bit of nostalgia, there's a lot to see: vintage Bentleys, Alfa Romeos and Jaguars rub shoulders with Norton motorbikes and Vespa scooters. Number plates and signs, jacks and oil cans take you back to the golden age of motoring. *Backbarrow (see websites for updates on telephone, price and opening hours). www. lakelandmotormuseum.co.uk.*

⑧ ★ Ulverston.
The home town of comic genius Stan Laurel makes much of its local hero; the Laurel and Hardy Museum is one of Ulverston's main attractions, along with the house where Stan was born.

This busy market town has some unusual attractions, as well as Stan Laurel's birthplace. Just outside the town is the unexpectedly peaceful Conishead Priory, a Buddhist retreat centre; the monks and nuns run the World Peace Café in the town centre, as a vegetarian and wholefood eatery. *For a full tour of Ulverston, see p 139.*

⑨ ★ South Lakes Animal Park.
A menagerie of creatures from many parts of the world makes this a must-see attraction for any animal-lover, especially if you have children in tow. Some of the animals roam free in large, naturalistic enclosures, and you might even meet a large ostrich on the path, while others, such as lions and bears, can be viewed from raised walkways. *For more information, see p 57, ④. Broughton Road, Dalton-in-Furness. ☎ 01229 466086. www.wildanimalpark.co.uk. Admission £11.50 adults; £8 children 3–15 yrs and seniors; free under 3 yrs; £1.50 friends of the park. Open Easter–Nov daily 10am–5pm; Nov–Easter daily 10am–4.30pm. Train to Dalton-in-Furness; bus X9 from Bowness and Windermere.*

A parrot poses for the camera at South Lakes Animal Park.

Where to **Stay & Dine**

The Armadale Hotel & Restaurant ULVERSTON A country house hotel a few miles north of Ulverston, The Armadale has several contemporary guestrooms and a Cumbrian restaurant. All the produce is sourced locally and the menu includes Cumberland sausage, lamb shank and mash, steak and ale pie and local mussels. *Arrad Foot, Nr Ulverston.* ☎ *01229 861257. thearmadale. co.uk. Doubles from £75. Entrees £8.95. Maestro, MC, V.*

The Aynsome Manor Hotel CARTMEL On the former estate of Cartmel Priory, this 16th-century manor house is now a country retreat. There are ten spacious traditional-style rooms, and a British menu with a few international twists. *Aynsome Lane, Cartmel.* ☎ *015395 36653. www.aynsomemanorhotel. co.uk. Doubles from £70. Menu from £25. AE, Maestro, MC, V.*

The Cavendish Arms CARTMEL This former coaching inn is over 450 years old with beamed ceilings and a roaring fire in winter, and ten comfortable guestrooms. The restaurant includes a choice of light bites, sandwiches, traditional Cumbrian main courses and the local favourite, sticky toffee pudding. *Cartmel.* ☎ *015395 35082. www.thecavendisharms.co.uk. Doubles from £60. Entrees £9.95. Maestro, MC, V.*

Hill Crest Country Guest House NEWBY BRIDGE This B&B lies just south of Newby Bridge and a short drive from Ulverston. There's a choice of individually decorated double, twin and family rooms, some with four-poster beds or decorative canopy curtains. The breakfasts are substantial and even include a choice of smoked haddock. *Brow Edge Road, Newby Bridge.* ☎ *015395 31766. www. hillcrest.gbr.cc. Doubles from £54. Maestro, MC, V.*

L'Enclume CARTMEL Book well ahead for this Michelin-starred restaurant in the village of Cartmel. Chef Simon Rogan's culinary creations whet the appetite and have critics bowing to his skills. Push the boat out and stay in one of their sleek contemporary guestrooms. *Cavendish Street, Cartmel.* ☎ *015395 36362. www.lenclume.co.uk. Doubles from £98. Menus £50–£90. AE, Maestro, MC, V.*

Netherwood Hotel GRANGE-OVER-SANDS This 19th-century former family home is a stylish coastal hotel overlooking Morecambe Bay. As well as traditional guestrooms, there's a restaurant serving local produce such as a Lakeland lamb and venison, and a spa with a heated indoor pool, fitness centre and beauty treatments. *Lindale Road, Grange-over-Sands.* ☎ *015395 32552. www.netherwood-hotel. co.uk. Doubles from £80. Menu £32. Maestro, MC, V.* ●

5 The Best Town Tours

Ambleside

1. The Armitt
2. Bridge House
3. The Apple Pie
4. Stock Ghyll Force
5. The Homes of Football
6. Waterhead Pier
7. Ambleside Roman Fort
8. Stagshaw Garden

Where to Stay & Dine

The Ambleside
Salutation Hotel **9**
Doi Imtanon **10**
The Glasshouse Restaurant **11**
Lakes Lodge **12**
The Log House **13**
Lucy's on a Plate **14**
Luigi's Restaurant **15**

The Priest Hole **16**
Rothay Manor Hotel **17**
Sheila's Cottage **18**
Skelwith Fold
Caravan Park **19**
Wateredge Inn **20**
Zeffirellis **21**

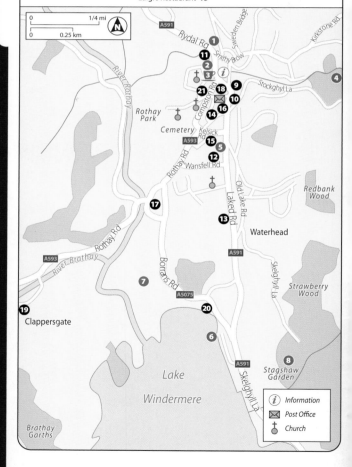

Information
Post Office
Church

Ambleside is a lively town at the north end of Windermere and a favourite base for visitors. While its present buildings are mostly Victorian, the original settlement is very much older: the Romans built a fort here in the 1st century. Remnants of ancient Galava can still be seen on the outskirts of town, while in the centre, the Armitt museum presents an unexpectedly diverting assortment of regional history and botany. Popular activities include boat trips from Waterhead Pier, shopping for outdoor gear and sampling a few pints in the local pubs. START: **Transport: by car A591/A593; by bus 505, 555.**

1 ★ The Armitt. This engaging combination of museum, gallery and library casts new light on local life and personalities. The Armitt is named after its founder, Louisa Armitt, who opened the museum in 1908 as a useful resource for the local scholarly community. It contains an eclectic collection of art and archaeology: Beatrix Potter's astonishingly detailed watercolours of fungi that showcase her talents as an artist; Bronze Age and Roman tools unearthed around Ambleside; John Ruskin's geological specimens and manuscripts; Victorian photographs of local scenes. *Rydal Road.* ☎ *015394 31212. http://fp.armitt. plus.com. Admission £3 adults, £2 concessions, £1 5-15 years, free under 5 years. Open daily 10am–5pm (last admission 4.30pm).*

2 ★★★ Bridge House. This is one of Ambleside's oldest and quaintest buildings, a literal bridge-house spanning Stock Ghyll, a tributary of the River Rothay. It's thought to have been built around 300 years ago as a summer house and apple store for the long-demolished Ambleside Hall. Today it's a National Trust information centre so you can go inside or take a photo from the pathway at the back. *Rydal Road.*

Take a Break

3 The Apple Pie. Next to the Bridge House, this café is a pillar of the Ambleside coffee-break scene. You can sample its famous apple pie or lemon cake while you're there, or buy it to take away for a picnic. *Rydal Road* ☎ *015394 33679.*

Time your visit right to Ambleside to avoid the crowds.

Ambleside's Outdoor Shops

Ambleside is renowned for its outdoor clothing and equipment shops. The biggest one is Gaynor Sports (www.gaynors.co.uk), where you can either spend a fortune on the most fashionable North Face windproof fleece or find a bargain in the basement among some of the lesser-known brands. Among several smaller stores are Lakes Climber/Lakes Runner and Adventure Peaks.

④ ★ Stock Ghyll Force. The path to this waterfall is steep in places, but it's only about a 15–20 minute walk from the Salutation Hotel. From the viewing point you can see two waterfalls merging into one, cascading some 70 feet into Stock Ghyll, which then flows down into the town below. It's particularly pretty here during springtime, when there's a carpet of daffodils in the woods. From the 14th century the ghyll powered local mills, reaching 12 at its peak, but they've all been demolished now or converted for other uses. *Stock Ghyll Lane.*

⑤ ★ The Homes of Football. Whenever I visit Ambleside, I pop into this gallery of large-scale photographs taken by artist Stuart Clarke. Many images give an insightful, sometimes repulsive and often humorous view of people at football matches, in England, Brazil and beyond. There are also photographs of music festivals, scenes of Cumbria and other locations. *100 Lake Road.* ☎ *015394 3444. www.homesoffootball.co.uk. Admission free (donations happily accepted). Open Thurs–Tues 10am–4.30pm.*

⑥ ★★ Waterhead Pier. This is Windermere's northern ferry terminal. Boat trips ply from here to Bowness, Lakeside and Brockhole. Park at the pier to visit Ambleside Roman Fort (see below). Several large hotels make the most of

The Armitt gives an insight into local history.

It's a short walk up to pretty Stock Ghyll.

the waterfront views. The Lakeside Hotel is a good bet for lunch. *North end of Skelghyll Lane. ☎ 015394 43360. www.windermere-lake cruises.co.uk. Tickets 24-hour Freedom of the Lake £11.60 adults; £5.80 children; £31.50 family. Timetable summer approx 9.15am–6.45pm; winter 10am–4.15pm (check timetable for individual routes). Bus 555.*

⑦ ★ Ambleside Roman Fort. The Romans first built this fort, which they named Galava, in Hadrian's time during the 1st or 2nd century AD to guard the road from Brougham to Ravenglass. The earliest structure was made of wood, but later a stone granary store was added and it became a supply base. *Borrans Road (park at Waterhead car park. www.english-heritage.org.uk. Admission free.*

Open daily sunrise to sunset. Bus 505/555.

⑧ ★ Stagshaw Garden. These pretty gardens are set on a hillside just south of Ambleside and were created by Cubby Acland, a former regional agent of the National Trust. Surrounded by woodland, the pathways wind through several acres, where visitors come to see the rhododendrons in full bloom from April to June. There are also some magnolia trees, camellias and small waterfalls, and superb views over Windermere and the fells beyond. *Just off Skelghyll Lane en route to Windermere. ☎ 015394 46027. www.nationaltrust.org.uk. Admission £2.50. Open Apr–Jun daily 10.30am–6.30pm. Bus 555/6, 599.*

Where to **Stay & Dine**

The Ambleside Salutation Hotel *BRITISH* This local landmark has traditional rooms and a reasonably priced restaurant with a menu using local produce. The bonus here is the health club, with its pool and

sauna. *Lake Road. ☎ 015394 32244. www.hotelslakedistrict.com. Doubles £82–£145. Restaurant open daily 12pm–2pm and 5.30pm–9pm. Mains from £7.95. AE, Maestro, MC, V.*

Sheila's Cottage is tucked away in a pretty side street.

Doi Imtanon *THAI* This ever-popular Thai restaurant in the former Market Hall is a good way to warm your insides after a day on the fells. Book ahead. *Market Place. ☎ 015394 32119. Open daily 7pm–10pm. Mains from £7.95. Maestro, MC, V.*

The Glasshouse Restaurant
MODERN BRITISH This restaurant's popularity soared after a triumphant appearance on Gordon Ramsay's *Kitchen Nightmares*. The menu is mostly British with an emphasis on Cumbrian produce and a few international twists. *Rydal Road. ☎ 015394 432137. www.theglasshouse restaurant.co.uk. Mains from £10.95. AE, Maestro, MC, V.*

Lakes Lodge Lakes Lodge is one of Ambleside's typical grey-stone properties, a three-storey house within minutes of local wining and dining. The rooms are painted in neutral tones with white bedding and modern, tiled bathrooms. Rooms at the back of the property have views over Ambleside. What's more, there's tight but ample parking for guests, a rarity around here. *Lakes Road. ☎ 015394 33240. www.lakes lodge.co.uk. Doubles from £140. AE, Maestro, MC, V.*

The Log House *MODERN BRITISH* The mouth-watering menu includes dishes like roasted Cumbrian lamb with crème-fraiche mash, and pan-fried seabass with sautéed potatoes. Upstairs, The Log House has three contemporary country guestrooms. *Lake Road. ☎ 015394 31077. www. loghouse.co.uk. Doubles £80–£90. Restaurant open Tues–Sun from 5pm. Mains from £14.95; menu £17.50. AE, Maestro, MC, V.*

Lucy's on a Plate *ENGLISH & EUROPEAN* Owned by the Lucy Cooks School in Staveley (p 52, **8**), this homely café and restaurant with pine tables and an open fire serves snacks, sandwiches and pasta during the day. At night, the lights are dimmed but it remains relaxed and unfussy with a daily changing menu of local produce and some international dishes. Save space for their huge array of tasty puddings such as Cumberland rum Nicky and apple-and-blackberry crumble. *Church Street. ☎ 015394 32288. www. lucysofambleside.co.uk. Open daily 10am–9m (last orders). Mains from £14. AE, Maestro, MC, V.*

Luigi's Restaurant *ITALIAN* For good home-style Italian cooking in Ambleside, you can't beat family-owned Luigi's. The chef adds his own tasty twist to traditional dishes and the waitress will suggest wines to complement them. Get here early to bag a window seat. *Kelsick Road.* ☎ *015394 33676. www.luigis-ambleside.co.uk. Open daily 6pm–10.30pm; seasonal variations. Mains from £11.95. AE, Maestro, MC, V.*

The Priest Hole *MEDITERRANEAN & ENGLISH* Next to the popular Royal Oak pub, this eatery has a small terrace. Inside, the tables are tucked into nooks and crannies, and the menu includes a mix of Spanish, Italian, Greek and locally inspired dishes. *Church Street.* ☎ *015394 33332. www.thepriesthole.co.uk. Open daily 11am–5pm and 6pm–10pm; seasonal variations. AE, Maestro, MC, V.*

Rothay Manor Hotel *FINE DINING* This Regency-style country manor house exudes luxury and comfort in a tranquil setting. Many of its individually styled guestrooms have balconies and garden views. Guests can use the nearby leisure club pool, spa and gym. It is renowned for afternoon tea and has an excellent restaurant. *Rothay Road, Ambleside.* ☎ *015394 33605. www.rothay manor.co.uk. Doubles £165–£335. Restaurant open lunch daily 12.30pm–1.45pm; afternoon tea 3.30pm–5pm; dinner 7.15pm–9pm. Menus £34–£46. AE, Maestro, MC, V.*

Sheila's Cottage *ENGLISH & INTERNATIONAL* This stone-fronted restaurant .is tucked away down a narrow lane, and has a cosy country feel with its wooden tables and open fire. The menu includes a mixture of Cumbrian specialities and international influences, such as Cumberland sausage or butternut risotto. *The Slack.* ☎ *015394 3379. Open daily 11am–9pm (last order). Mains from £9.50. AE, Maestro, MC, V.*

Skelwith Fold Caravan Park On the Hawkshead side of Ambleside, this is a family caravan site with a kids'

playground, sports pitch, launderette and shop. Bring your own touring caravan or rent one of the site's static models. *Rydal Road, Skelwith.* ☎ *015394 31212. www. skelwithfold.co.uk. Caravan pitch £18–£23/night, £115–£145/week. Maestro, MC, V.*

Wateredge Inn *BRITISH* This family-run B&B is set on the northern shore of Windermere, about a 20-minute walk from Ambleside town centre. But with a waterside garden, gastro-pub food and a bar, you may not want to stray far. Dogs welcome, space permitting. *Rydal Road.* ☎ *015394 32332. www. wateredgeinn.co.uk. Doubles £90–£140. Restaurant open 12pm–4pm and 5pm–9pm. Mains from £7.95. AE, Maestro, MC, V.*

Zeffirellis *ITALIAN* Arthouse cinema, jazz bar, café and restaurant all in one, this imaginative concept caters for a wide-ranging clientele. The menu includes fresh pasta and casseroles as well as pizzas with smaller portions of everything for kids. You can dine in the Jazz Bar, where there is live music on Friday and Saturday nights (no under 16s after 9pm). *Compston Road.* ☎ *015394 33845. www.zeffirellis. com. Restaurant open daily 5.30pm–10pm; bar 4pm–late (food until 9pm). Mains from £7.75. Maestro, MC, V.*

Ambleside is renowned for its outdoor equipment and clothing stores.

Bowness-on-Windermere

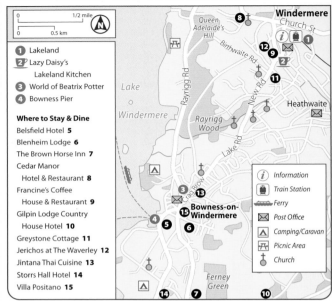

0   1/2 mile
0   0.5 km

1 Lakeland
2 Lazy Daisy's
  Lakeland Kitchen
3 World of Beatrix Potter
4 Bowness Pier

Where to Stay & Dine
Belsfield Hotel 5
Blenheim Lodge 6
The Brown Horse Inn 7
Cedar Manor
  Hotel & Restaurant 8
Francine's Coffee
  House & Restaurant 9
Gilpin Lodge Country
  House Hotel 10
Greystone Cottage 11
Jerichos at The Waverley 12
Jintana Thai Cuisine 13
Storrs Hall Hotel 14
Villa Positano 15

Windermere

i Information
🚆 Train Station
⛴ Ferry
✉ Post Office
⛺ Camping/Caravan
🏕 Picnic Area
✝ Church

Lakeside Bowness-on-Windermere is joined at the hip with the railhead town of Windermere. Merging almost seamlessly, these form the largest and busiest destinations in the Lake District. Windermere was put on the map by the arrival of the railway and its pretty stone buildings are mostly Victorian. Bowness was originally a much older settlement clustered round a 15th-century church. Today, tourism fuels the local economy, and many galleries and boutiques vie for attention. All around the lake, holiday homes and palatial hotels lie half-hidden in dense woodland. The waterfront is a hive of activity all summer long, as boats buzz back and forth, spilling visitors out on the grassy banks. START: **Lakeland. Transport: train to Windermere station; bus 555.**

1 ★ Lakeland. This is the original HQ/anchor store of the well-known mail-order houseware firm, now a national chain selling must-have kitchen gadgets and innovative household products. Fill your shopping trolley with magic oven liners, cunning storage solutions and digital luggage scales! It has an excellent in-store café. *Alexandra Buildings, Windermere station.* ☎ *015394 88100. www.lakeland. co.uk. Open Mon–Fri 8am–7pm; Sat 9am–6pm; Sun 11am–5pm; bank holidays 9am–5pm.*

Visitors pour into Bowness, especially during peak season.

Take a Break

2 Lazy Daisy's Lakeland Kitchen. Tuck into steak-filled ciabatta rolls, cheese and chutney sandwiches and sticky cakes during the day. Come back at night for a heartier range of fresh fish, meat and vegetarian dishes with a bottle of wine. *31–33 Crescent Road, Windermere ☎ 015394 43877. Open daily 9.30am–9pm.*

3 ★★★ kids World of Beatrix Potter. Lose yourself (or your offspring) in the unthreatening world of Jeremy Fisher and Peter Rabbit. There's a shop full of Potter-related merchandise and a café-restaurant. *For more information, see p 30,* bullet **1**. *Bowness-on-Windermere. ☎ 015394 88444. www.hop-skip-jump.com. Admission £6 adults; £3 children. Open daily summer 10am–5.30pm; winter 10am–4.30pm.*

4 ★ Bowness Pier. Along the lakefront, swans join tourists admiring the views. This is Windermere's biggest terminal for boat tours of the lake and islands (see Windermere Lake Cruises p 12, **1**). There are trips to and from Ambleside and Lakeside, and to Ferry House, the route to Beatrix Potter's house, Hill Top. You can also hire canoes. The grand Belsfield Hotel overlooking the pier is a good bet for afternoon tea, served outside in good weather (see below p 104). *Bowness Pier. ☎ 015394 43360.*

Lazing on a Sunny Afternoon

Bowness and Windermere offer plenty of gentle shopping, eating and leisure activities. Both have lots of little art and craft galleries, gift shops and boutiques, while the Lakeland store by Windermere station makes an interesting diversion for all but the resolutely undomesticated visitor. Stop for tea at the Belsfield Hotel, munch some chips by the pier, then work off a few calories with a lakeside walk, a bike ride, a spot of canoeing or sailing (p 104).

It's easy to relax on Bowness' waterfront.

*www.windermere-lakecruises.co.uk.
Tickets 24-hour Freedom of the Lake
£11.60 adults; £5.80 children; £31.50
family. Timetable summer approx*

*9.15am–6.45pm; winter 10am–
4.15pm (check timetable for individual routes).*

Where to **Stay & Dine**

Belsfield Hotel *MODERN
EUROPEAN* Set back from the lake
within six acres of gardens, this
hotel has lake views, four-poster
beds or family rooms. There's an
indoor heated pool and sauna,
snooker room and putting green, as
well as a terrace (open in summer)
and restaurant, which serves a
3-course dinner. *Kendal Road, Bowness-on-Windermere.* ☎ 015394
42448. www.corushotels.com/
belsfield. Doubles from £81. Restaurant 6.30pm–9pm. Menu £21. AE,
Maestro, MC, V.*

Blenheim Lodge An 11-room
B&B overlooking National Trust
woodland, Blenheim Lodge has
cosy comfortable rooms with floral
curtains and antique-look furnishings. *Brentfell Road, Bowness-on-
Windermere.* ☎ 015394 43440.

*www.blenheim-lodge.com. Doubles
£80–£120. Maestro, MC, V.*

The Brown Horse Inn *BRITISH*
For traditional pub food, try this welcoming inn a couple of miles from
Bowness. You can tuck into hearty
plates of venison, pheasant and
lamb from the Brown Horse Estate,
and wash them down with local
ales. There's also a farm shop here.
Winster, Bowness-on-Windermere.
☎ 015394 43443. www.thebrown
horseinn.co.uk. Restaurant open
daily 12pm–2pm and 6pm–9pm.
Mains from £12.50. Maestro, MC, V.*

Cedar Manor Hotel & Restaurant *BRITISH* Guestrooms and
suites are individually designed with
pine furnishings and floral textiles.
Downstairs, the award-winning restaurant uses seasonal produce to

create an inspired menu such as beef fillet with fondant potato or game suet pudding with spiced poached pear. *Ambleside Road, Windermere.* ☎ *015394 43192. www.cedarmanor.co.uk. Doubles from £96. Restaurant open daily 6.30pm–8.30pm (last orders). Mains from £12.95. AE, Maestro, MC, V.*

Francine's Coffee House & Restaurant *MODERN EUROPEAN*
Francine's deftly combines a Cumbrian and continental menu from breakfast through to dinner. Enjoy Cumberland sausage or croissant for breakfast, Greek salad for lunch and fresh mussels or duck breast for dinner. *27 Main Road, Windermere.* ☎ *015394 44088. www.francines restaurantwindermere.co.uk. Open Tues–Sun 10am–4.30pm and Wed–Sun 6.30pm–11.30pm. Mains from £8.95. Maestro, MC, V.*

Gilpin Lodge Country House Hotel *MODERN BRITISH* This elegantly decorated country house hotel offers a little luxury away from the madding crowds of Windermere; the stylish, individually designed guestrooms each have their own seating areas. There are also spa treatments and a splendid restaurant serving scallops, monkfish, venison and other modern classics. *Crook Road, Windermere.* ☎ *015394 88818. www.gilpinlodge. co.uk. Doubles £145–£220. Restaurant open daily lunch 12pm–2pm; light bites until 5pm; afternoon tea 3pm–5.30pm; dinner 6.30pm–9.15pm. AE, Maestro, MC, V.*

Greystone Cottage Built in typical Lakeland stone, this small Victorian B&B is centrally placed just a few minutes' walk from Windermere station. It offers bright, clean accommodation in a peaceful and homely atmosphere. *6 Ellerthwaite Road, Windermere.* ☎ *015394 46907. www.greystone-cottage.*

co.uk. Doubles £47–£60. Maestro, MC, V.

Jerichos at The Waverley
MODERN BRITISH Award-winning chef Chris Blaydes produces creative cuisine. Enjoy steak nights, Flookburgh shrimps or Scotch beef, and stay in the contemporary guestrooms on-site. *College Road, Windermere.* ☎ *015394 42522. www. jerichos.co.uk. Restaurant open Fri–Wed 7pm–9.30pm (last orders). Mains from £15.25. Maestro, MC, V.*

Jintana Thai Cuisine *THAI* Exotic with mellow lighting, Jintana's is a relaxed Thai restaurant. Choose classic Thai green curry or try their pan-fried salmon fillet with creamy coconut sauce. *Lake Road, Bowness.* ☎ *015394 45002. Open daily 5pm–10pm (10.30pm Fri and Sat). Menus £11.95. AE, Maestro, MC, V.*

Storrs Hall Hotel *MODERN BRITISH* Located south of Bowness overlooking Lake Windermere, this is a luxury Grade II Georgian mansion with huge rooms dressed in period-style English furnishings. Its opulent facilities include extensive grounds and access to a leisure club at the Low Wood Hotel. This is quite a formal hotel and is not suitable for children under 12 years. *Just off the A592 at Storrs.* ☎ *015394 47111. www.elh.co.uk. Doubles £92–£320. Restaurant open 12.30pm–2pm and 7pm–9pm. Menu £42.50. AE, Maestro, MC, V.*

Villa Positano *ITALIAN* This long-established Italian restaurant in the middle of Bowness is popular for its easy-going atmosphere and family-friendly menu. As well as pizza and pasta, you'll find steaks, chicken and vegetable dishes to choose from. Book ahead during peak season. *Ash Street.* ☎ *015394 45663. Open daily 5.30pm–10pm. Mains from £5.95. Maestro, MC, V.*

Cockermouth

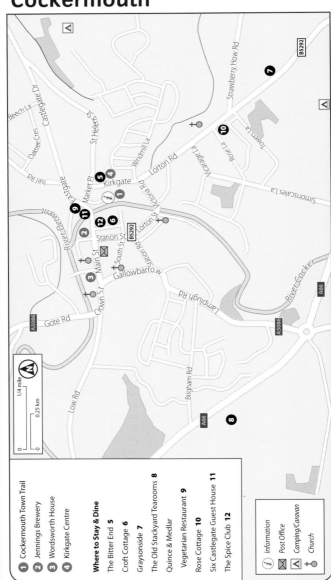

1 Cockermouth Town Trail
2 Jennings Brewery
3 Wordsworth House
4 Kirkgate Centre

Where to Stay & Dine

The Bitter End **5**
Croft Cottage **6**
Graysonside **7**
The Old Stackyard Tearooms **8**
Quince & Medlar
Vegetarian Restaurant **9**
Rose Cottage **10**
Six Castlegate Guest House **11**
The Spice Club **12**

i Information
☒ Post Office
◪ Camping/Caravan
✝ Church

I **have a soft spot for Cockermouth, as it is quieter than many Lakeland towns** so shop owners have more time to chat and it's easier to take in the Georgian architecture at a gentle pace. After the Romans built a camp at the confluence of the rivers Derwent and Cocker, little happened until the Normans built a castle between the two rivers in the 12th century. From this time, the town grew up around the textile industry, spreading south of the castle. Today the castle ruins are on private property and rarely open to the public, but you can visit Wordsworth's birthplace and Jennings Brewery, several studios and art galleries and the Kirkgate Centre, a hub of performing arts and music. START: **Cockermouth tourist office, Market Street. Transport: bus X4, X5, 217, 600.**

❶ ★ **Cockermouth Town Trail.** Call in at the tourist office on Market Street to pick up a copy of the Town Trail, devised by the local Civic Trust. As well as pointing out the most popular attractions, this circular walk takes you past some lesser-known gems, like the former Rope Walk, where the ropemakers used to work, a hat factory now turned into apartments, weavers' cottages and workshops and the Mayo Statue, commemorating the town's former Member of Parliament assassinated while serving as Viceroy of India. *Tourist Information Centre, Market Street.* ☎ *01900 822634.*

❷ ★★★ **Jennings Brewery.** Visitors are introduced to the brewing process with a film and a tour. The brewery was founded in 1828 by John Jennings Sr, and moved to its present location in 1874. Today it is part of the Marston's group. It has its own well, which provides a distinctive taste to its ales. The most famous of Jennings' beers are Snecklifter and Cocker Hoop, but they also brew seasonal ales, which you can try at the end of the tour and then buy in the shop. *Castle Brewery.* ☎ *0845 1297185. www. jenningsbrewery.co.uk. Admission £5.50 adults; £2.50 12–18 yrs. Tours Jan–Feb, Nov–Dec Mon–Fri 2pm; Sat 11am and 2pm; Mar–Jun and*

Sept–Oct Mon–Sat 11am and 2pm; Jul–Aug daily 11am and 2pm.

❸ ★ **Wordsworth House.** As the poet's birthplace, Cockermouth is an important stop on the Wordsworth trail. The house where he was born in 1770 is now owned and managed by the National Trust, and although it no longer contains many original furnishings or artefacts, it has been restored to provide an authentic insight into late 18th-century décor and lifestyle. Costumed actors re-enact the roles of household staff of the period, and can answer questions about the house

Follow the town trail around Georgian Cockermouth.

Wordsworth was born at this house in Cockermouth.

from the kitchen to the bedrooms—early visitors may be able to watch bread-making in the kitchen. You can also explore the garden, which has been replanted with vegetables, herbs and wildflowers as it would have been during Wordsworth's time (p 35). *Main Street, Cockermouth.* ☎ *01900 820884. www.wordsworthhouse.org.uk. Admission £5.90 adults; £2.90 children; £14.70 family. Open Apr–Nov Mon–Sat 11am–5pm.*

It's easy to find your way round Cockermouth.

④ ★ **Kirkgate Centre.** This Victorian property once housed a school but after having remained derelict for several years, it was saved from demolition by a collective local effort and opened as an arts centre in 1995. It now plays a key role in the town's cultural life, with a cinema/theatre run by volunteers. Along with film screenings, the Kirkgate hosts an impressive line-up of theatre, music and visual arts that brings more than a few celebrities to Cockermouth's doors. *Kirkgate. Box office* ☎ *01900 826448. www.thekirkgate.com.*

Where to **Stay & Dine**

The Bitter End Traditional pub-grub fare such as jacket potatoes, steaks and scampi is on offer at this well-liked inn, which also takes a pride in its range of real ales. It has a different regional guest beer each week. *15 Kirkgate.* ☎ *01900 828993. www.bitterend.co.uk. Open for food 12pm–2pm and 6pm–8.45pm. Mains from £8.95. Maestro, MC, V.*

Croft Cottage This renovated Georgian townhouse in the heart of Cockermouth has a traditional lounge with a bare stone wall, contrasting with modern en suite guestrooms painted white with purple-and-maroon feature walls and complementary textiles. As well as double and twin rooms, there's a family room available. *6–8 Challoner Street. ☎ 01900 827533. www. croft-guesthouse.com. Doubles from £65. AE, Maestro, MC, V.*

Graysonside Located just outside Cockermouth, Graysonside offers modern, comfortable en suite accommodation or self-catering for two in a converted stone barn. *Lorton Road. ☎ 01900 822351. www.graysonside.co.uk. Doubles £70, s/c £350. Maestro, MC, V.*

The Old Stackyard Tearooms *BRITISH* Located just outside Cockermouth at Wellington Farm, this café is the ideal place to indulge in home-baked cakes and sandwiches. It's also home to Wellington Jerseys ice cream, so you can indulge in scoops of butterscotch ripple crunch, cointreau and orange and other flavours. *Wellington Farm ☎ 01900 822777. www.wellington jerseys.co.uk. Open daily 10am–5pm. Mains from £5.50.*

Quince & Medlar Vegetarian Restaurant This acclaimed vegetarian restaurant needs booking ahead, the chefs trained at the Michelin-starred hotel-restaurant Sharrow Bay. The menu, which changes every two months, includes wholesome, inventive dishes like butternut and broad beans with coconut, almonds and tomato. *13 Castlegate. ☎ 01900 823579. www.quinceandmedlar.co.uk. Open Tues–Sat 7pm–9.30pm (last orders). Mains from £13.95. Maestro, MC, V.*

Enjoy curry favourites at The Spice Club in Cockermouth.

Rose Cottage This cottage on the outskirts of Cockermouth offers en suite B&B accommodation with contemporary furnishings. Ground-floor rooms and family rooms are available. *Lorton Road. ☎ 01900 822189. www.rosecottageguest. co.uk. Doubles £60–£80; dinner, b&b doubles £80–£120. Maestro, MC, V.*

Six Castlegate Guest House This Grade II-listed Georgian town house has been immaculately refurbished, with individually styled guestrooms decorated in neutral tones. *Six Castlegate. ☎ 01900 826786. www.sixcastlegate.co.uk. Doubles from £65. Maestro, MC, V.*

The Spice Club *INDIAN & BANGLADESHI* You can eat in or take away at this Bangladeshi-owned restaurant in the town centre, which serves a lengthy menu of popular classics including Tandoori, balti and massala dishes. *25 Main Street ☎ 01900 828288. Open daily 6pm–11pm. Mains from £7.95. Maestro, MC, V.*

Coniston

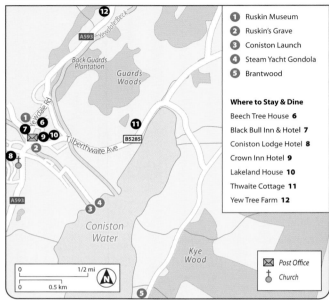

1. Ruskin Museum
2. Ruskin's Grave
3. Coniston Launch
4. Steam Yacht Gondola
5. Brantwood

Where to Stay & Dine

Beech Tree House **6**
Black Bull Inn & Hotel **7**
Coniston Lodge Hotel **8**
Crown Inn Hotel **9**
Lakeland House **10**
Thwaite Cottage **11**
Yew Tree Farm **12**

✉ Post Office
✝ Church

C oniston stands at the north-western edge of Coniston Water, beneath the fell known as the Old Man of Coniston. A copper-mining area since Norman times, Coniston became a popular resort in the mid-19th century when the Furness Railway arrived. It became famous through its associations with the art critic John Ruskin, the world water-speed record-breaker Donald Campbell and *Swallows and Amazons* author Arthur Ransome, who all had connections with the area. START: **Ruskin Museum. Transport: bus X12, 505.**

Take in the ever-expanding Campbell exhibits at the John Ruskin Museum.

❶ ★ **Ruskin Museum.** Set up by John Ruskin's former secretary, W. G. Collingwood, in 1901, this museum contains several of Ruskin's manuscripts, **sketchbooks and paintings** as well as sculptures and portraits. The museum also has some Stone Age axe heads and sections on **local geology** and the copper-mining and textile industries (linen and lace-making were once important cottage industries around Coniston). Another highlight is Arthur Ransome's dinghy *Mavis* and, from 2010, Donald Campbell's reconstructed *Bluebird K7* will be on display in the new **Bluebird Wing**. *Yewdale Road.* ☎ *015394 41164. www.ruskinmuseum.com. Admission £7 adults; £3.50 children. Open winter Wed–Sun 10.30am–3.30pm; summer daily 10am–5.30pm.*

2 ★ Ruskin's Grave. Ruskin's final resting place is in the cemetery of St Andrew's Church. His grave lies towards the back of the church-yard in a shady spot, marked by a large Celtic cross made of local green slate from the Tiberthwaite quarry. It was designed by Ruskin's secretary, W. G. Collingwood, and carved by H. T. Miles. *Yewdale Road.* ☎ *015394 41262.*

3 ★ Coniston Launch. You can take various themed boat trips from the pier, including one called *Swallows and Amazons* and another tour entitled *Campbells on Coniston*. It is possible to combine lakeshore walks with boat trips from Coniston, Waterhead (Ambleside) or Torver (southwest of Conis-ton village). Launches also usually stop at John Ruskin's house, Brantwood, on the eastern shore (p 112, **5**). *Coniston Pier/Boat House. www.conistonlaunch. co.uk. Admission northern cruise £7.90 adults; £3.95 children 3–16 yrs; £20 family; combined tickets available. Open Mar–beginning Nov daily*

Art critic and social thinker John Ruskin is central to the Ruskin Museum.

10.15am–5.45pm; Nov–Mar week-ends only 10.25am–3.10pm—check for complete timetable. Bus 505 from Windermere and Ambleside.

4 ★ Steam Yacht Gondola. This magnificently restored Victo-rian steam yacht run by the National Trust is an elegant alternative to the conventional launches on Coniston Water. *Gondola* was originally launched in 1859. A violent storm left the boat unusable in the 1960s, but the National Trust renovated it and by 1980 it was ready to sail once again. The boat carries over 80 passengers and is sumptuously fitted with upholstered saloon seating. Rather than the traditional coal fuel, the boat uses sustainable logs made from wood waste. *Gondola* sails silently and smoothly across the lake from Coniston pier to Brant-wood and Monk Coniston (on the northern shore).

John Ruskin is buried in Coniston.

John Ruskin

Born in London in 1819, John Ruskin was the son of a sherry merchant. His father introduced him to painting and poetry, while his deeply religious Calvinist mother schooled him rigorously in Bible studies. He went to **Christ Church Oxford** and immersed himself in geology, art and architecture. Bucking the critical trends of the time, his appreciation of the genius of William Turner led to his five-volume series *Modern Painters* (1843–60). Ruskin was a considerable artist in his own right. He sketched profusely and later became the **first Slade Professor of Art** at Oxford (1869–79).

In 1848, he married Effie Gray, but the marriage was not a happy one and she left him six years later for the Pre-Raphaelite painter John Everett Millais. From the 1850s onwards, Ruskin became increasingly preoccupied with social justice and the inequities of the Victorian age. He gave away most of his inheritance, and famously wrote in one of his essays **'There is no wealth, but life'**. He died in 1900, aged 81, leaving behind thousands of sketches, watercolours and volumes of writing.

Trips may be cancelled in poor weather. As with the launches, you can buy combined boat- and Brantwood tickets, and boat-and-walk trips. *Coniston Pier/Boat House. www.nationaltrust.org.uk. Admission £1.50–£7 adults; £1–£3 children; £17.50 family. Open approx daily 10.30am–5pm—check for full timetable. Bus 505 from Windermere and Ambleside.*

5 ★★ **Brantwood.** John Ruskin bought Brantwood in 1872 and added his own extensions to it, transforming it into a fitting repository for his many art treasures. One of his most notable additions was the dining room with views of the lake and the Coniston fells. After exploring the house, you can wander round the extensive garden of flowers, herbs, fruit, trees, bridges and streams, and then relax in the café outside. The car park at Brantwood is small, so during high season it's easier to take a boat from Coniston. *Coniston.* ☎ *015394 41396. www.brantwood.org.uk. Admission £5.95 adults; £4.50 students; £1.20 children; £4 gardens only; £11.95 family; there are also combined bus, boat and Brantwood tickets. Open mid-Mar–mid-Nov daily 11am–5.30pm; mid-Nov–mid-Mar daily 11.30am–4.30pm. Launch or Gondola to Brantwood.*

Where to **Stay & Dine**

Beech Tree House Just out of the village centre, this B&B has pretty gardens, individually styled rooms and off-road parking.

Yewdale Road. ☎ *015394 41717. Doubles £52–£66. Cash and cheque only.*

Sample some local ales at The Black Bull in Coniston.

Black Bull Inn & Hotel *BRITISH* The Black Bull is many things in one: a restaurant, pub and micro-brewery, as well as having accommodation upstairs. Tuck into traditional pub food from jacket potatoes to breaded scampi, and enjoy local Coniston Brewing Company ales such as Bluebird Bitter. *Coppermines Road.* ☎ *015394 41335. www. conistonbrewery.com. Open daily 12pm–11pm (food until 9pm) Mains from £7.75. Maestro, MC, V.*

Coniston Lodge Hotel This is a country-style hotel with a mixture of twin, double and family rooms, some with four-poster beds but all dressed with floral textiles. *Sunny Brow.* ☎ *015394 41201. www. coniston-lodge.com. Doubles £95–£118. Maestro, MC, V.*

Crown Inn Hotel *BRITISH* A traditional Lakeland pub with B&B accommodation, the rooms are compact but comfortable. Downstairs, the pub serves Cumberland sausage and mash with onion gravy and other local favourites. *Tiberthwaite Avenue.* ☎ *015394 41243. www.crown innconiston.com. Doubles £90. Bar open daily 12pm–11pm (food until 9pm). Mains from £8. AE, Maestro, MC, V.*

Lakeland House Set in the heart of Coniston village with the fells rising dramatically behind it, this refurbished hotel has individually styled modern en suite rooms and an Internet café. There's space to store bicycles; packed lunches on request. *Tiberthwaite Avenue.* ☎ *015394 41303. www.lakelandhouse.co.uk. Doubles £60–£70. Maestro, MC, V.*

Thwaite Cottage This traditional Lakeland cottage is a ten-minute stroll from the village in a wooded setting close to Coniston Water. It has three country-style rooms and a log fire in the lounge. *Waterhead.* ☎ *015394 41367. www.thwaite cottage.co.uk. Doubles £60–£72. Cash and cheque only.*

Yew Tree Farm *BRITISH* Owned by Beatrix Potter in the 1930s, this B&B featured as Hill Top Farm in the 2006 film *Miss Potter*. Surrounded by the Furness Fells, it has immaculate guestrooms with bespoke beds. There's also a tearoom for guests and passing visitors; farm-raised heritage meat is on sale, including Herdwick lamb. *Coniston.* ☎ *015394 41433. www.yewtree-farm.com. Doubles £104–£124. Tearoom open Easter–Oct daily 11am–4pm; Oct–Easter Sat and Sun 11am–4pm (closed 29th Dec–2nd Jan). Mains from £5.95. AE, Maestro, MC, V.*

Grasmere

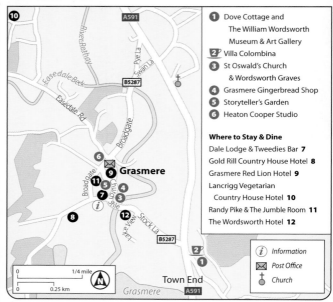

1. Dove Cottage and The William Wordsworth Museum & Art Gallery
2. Villa Colombina
3. St Oswald's Church & Wordsworth Graves
4. Grasmere Gingerbread Shop
5. Storyteller's Garden
6. Heaton Cooper Studio

Where to Stay & Dine
Dale Lodge & Tweedies Bar **7**
Gold Rill Country House Hotel **8**
Grasmere Red Lion Hotel **9**
Lancrigg Vegetarian Country House Hotel **10**
Randy Pike & The Jumble Room **11**
The Wordsworth Hotel **12**

(i) Information
✉ Post Office
† Church

W illiam Wordsworth described Grasmere as 'the loveliest spot that man hath ever found'. It gets fiendishly busy on fine bank holidays and during peak holiday periods. In summer, the Rushbearing ceremony and the Grasmere sports attract large crowds, **but there's usually an exodus in the late afternoons as day trippers head home.** Time your visit for a pleasant stroll round its attractions, especially the lake and local galleries and gift shops. START: Dove Cottage. Transport: bus 599.

1 ★ Dove Cottage and The William Wordsworth Museum & Art Gallery. Dove Cottage was home to the Lake District's best-known poet from 1799 to 1808. Visits to the house are by informative timed tours, which provide a fascinating insight into his life in Grasmere. The museum and gallery next door has a permanent exhibition of watercolours, portraits and manuscripts from the Romantic era, and hosts temporary exhibitions

throughout the year. *A591 at Town End.* ☎ *015394 35544. www. wordsworth.org.uk. Admission includes cottage and gallery £7.50 adults; £4.50 children; free under 6 yrs; £17.50 family (1–2 adults, 1–3 children). Open daily 9.30am–5.30pm (last admission 5pm).*

Take a Break

2 Villa Colombina. In the summer months you can relax outdoors

Wordsworth lived at Dove Cottage for several years.

with a refreshing drink or snack. At night the café turns into an Italian restaurant, which is spacious enough to cater for large groups. *Town End.* ☎ *015394 35268. www. howfoot.co.uk/menu. Open daily 10am–5pm, 6pm–8.45pm (9pm in summer). Mains from £8.50.*

③ ★ St Oswald's Church & Wordsworth Graves. The first church was built here in the mid-7th century by King Oswald of Northumbria, who was said to have descended from the pagan god Woden. Oswald became a Christian convert and was venerated as a saint soon after his death. The present church of St Oswald's dates from the 13th century and was remodelled in the 19th. Every July, the ceremony known as Rushbearing takes place, and rushes are laid in the church, commemorating an old method of purifying the air and providing insulation. This became unnecessary after flagstones were laid in the aisle in the 19th century but the tradition still continues.

Most visitors come to see the Wordsworth family graves in the cemetery. There's a memorial to William Wordsworth in the nave of the church. *Church Stile. Open daily 9am–5pm.*

④ ★ Grasmere Gingerbread Shop. This shop beside St Oswald's Church was founded by the enterprising Sarah Nelson in the 19th century. She rented Gate Cottage and began making gingerbread. This soon caught on with passing Victorian tourists, and has been a roaring success ever since. Since she died in 1904, the shop has changed hands several times but little has changed, including Sarah's delicious recipe. *Church Cottage.* ☎ *015394 35428. www.grasmeregingerbread. co.uk. Open Mon–Sat 9.15am– 5.30pm; Sun 12.30pm–5.30pm.*

Wordsworth fell in love with the beauty of Grasmere.

Wordsworth is buried in St Oswald's cemetery.

5 ★ Storyteller's Garden. The garden is run by pioneering English storyteller Taffy Thomas, who started Tales in Trust, stories entrusted to him by traditional performers who inspire him. Throughout the year there are regular themed events, all of which involve a story, from Easter to Rushbearing to Halloween and Christmas—it's not just for kids but more of a storytelling performance, sometimes with help from musicians and jugglers. *Church Stile.* ☎ *015394 35641. www.taffy thomas.co.uk.*

6 ★ Heaton Cooper Studio. This family-run gallery was opened in 1938 by local artist William Heaton. It presents original Lake District landscape paintings by both Alfred and his son William Heaton, as well as works by several of their descendents. You can browse or purchase the paintings, as well as Lake District prints and cards. *Broadgate.* ☎ *015394 35280. www.heaton cooper.co.uk. Open Mon–Sat 9am–5pm.*

Where to **Stay & Dine**

Dale Lodge & Tweedies Bar
The rooms at this refurbished Georgian building are dressed with rustic wooden furnishings, or you can opt for the luxury mews accommodation, complete with hot tub. There's an intimate restaurant on-site and a traditional pub with a large garden. *Red Bank Road.* ☎ *015394 35300. www.dalelodgehotel.co.uk. Doubles £90–£440. Maestro, MC, V.*

Gold Rill Country House Hotel
BRITISH Just two minutes from the centre of the village, this country house hotel has views of the lake and the nearby fells. The rooms are contemporary and stylish in muted greens and browns. There's a large restaurant with lake views where you can enjoy fine Cumbrian fare. *Red Bank Road.* ☎ *015394 35486. www.goldrill.co.uk. Doubles*

£94–£240, Restaurant open 7pm (one service), menu £27. Maestro, MC, V.

Grasmere Red Lion Hotel This hotel places an emphasis on comfort and simplicity, with spacious rooms in pastel tones and a restaurant that uses seasonal produce and will cater for any dietary requirements. It also boasts a leisure centre with a mini-gym, steam room and sauna. *Red Lion Square.* ☎ *015394 35456. www. grasmereredlionhotel.co.uk. Doubles £112–£150. AE, Maestro, MC, V.*

Lancrigg Vegetarian Country House Hotel *VEGETARIAN* Just half a mile outside Grasmere, this rambling country house hotel has a range of guestrooms, some luxury four-posters, others more homely in style. Each one is named after personalities or places associated with the house. The restaurant presents

Lake Artists Summer Exhibition

The Lake Artists Society was founded over a century ago in 1904 by local artist and historian (and secretary to John Ruskin, p 112), W. G. Collingwood. Each year, it holds a summer exhibition in Grasmere Village Hall just off Broadgate, from late July to early September. The early exhibitions consisted mostly of landscapes, but today, the exhibits are more varied, although most of the member artists are based locally. www.lakeartists.org.uk.

organic, vegetarian dishes like tofu burger or Cajun-spiced aubergines. *Easedale.* ☎ *015394 35317. www. lancrigg.co.uk. Doubles £170–£210, Restaurant open breakfast 8.30am–10am; lunch 12pm–5pm; dinner 6.30pm–8pm. Opening flexible, so best to book. Mains from £12. Maestro, MC, V.*

Randy Pike & The Jumble Room *MODERN BRITISH* A luxury B&B with two ultra-modern suites, the Randy Pike is just a short distance from Ambleside. Their restaurant, The Jumble Room, does good home-cooking using local produce and with an international slant, such as roasted corn-fed chicken with pea and courgette risotto. *Off the B5286 between Outgate and Pull Woods.* ☎ *015394 36088. www.randypike. co.uk. Suites £180–£200. Entrees from £13.50. Maestro, MC, V.*

The Wordsworth Hotel *MODERN BRITISH* Set in the heart of Grasmere within two acres of landscaped gardens, this upmarket hotel has high-quality upholstered chairs and furnishings and a range of leisure facilities, including a heated indoor pool, sauna and mini gym. The Prelude Restaurant, named after one of Wordsworth's works, has a seasonal menu, while the bistro takes a more casual approach with light bites, sandwiches and coffees. *Stock Lane.* ☎ *015394 35592. www.the*

wordsworthhotel.co.uk. Doubles £110–£140. Restaurant/bistro lunch daily 12pm–2pm; dinner 7pm–9pm (Fri–Sat 9.30pm). Menu £39.50; bistro mains £9.95. AE, Maestro, MC, V.

Villa Colombina Next to Dove Cottage, this café-restaurant has a few tables outside as well as ample space indoors. The vast menu includes risotto, pasta, pizza and Italian chicken, meat and fish dishes. *Town End.* ☎ *015394 35268. www. howfoot.co.uk/menu. Open daily 10am–5pm, 6pm–8.45pm (9pm in summer). Mains from £8.50.*

The Wordsworth Hotel in Grasmere has a spa and a restaurant.

Hawkshead

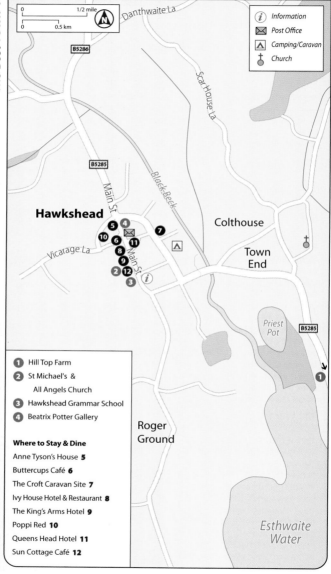

0 · 1/2 mile
0 · 0.5 km

Danthwaite La

B5286

Scar House La

B5285

Main St

Black Beck

Hawkshead

Colthouse

Vicarage La

Town
End

Priest
Pot

B5285

Roger
Ground

Esthwaite
Water

(i) Information
⊠ Post Office
▲ Camping/Caravan
✝ Church

1. Hill Top Farm
2. St Michael's &
   All Angels Church
3. Hawkshead Grammar School
4. Beatrix Potter Gallery

Where to Stay & Dine

Anne Tyson's House **5**
Buttercups Café **6**
The Croft Caravan Site **7**
Ivy House Hotel & Restaurant **8**
The King's Arms Hotel **9**
Poppi Red **10**
Queens Head Hotel **11**
Sun Cottage Café **12**

I t is easy to understand why visitors flock to this exceptionally pretty village. Cobbled streets and courtyards, flower boxes and specialist shops, cottages and pubs all add up to an idyllic Lakeland scene. Hawkshead was an important centre for wool in the Middle Ages, but more recent claims to fame include associations with William Wordsworth and Beatrix Potter. START: **Hill Top Farm, Nr Sawrey. Transport: boat to ferry house and walk or bus 525 to Hawkshead.**

① ★★★ Hill Top Farm. The house where Beatrix Potter wrote many of her famous animal tales lies 2 miles/3.2 km from Hawkshead in the village of Near Sawrey. It's a typical 17th-century Lakeland dwelling with small rooms and a rambling cottage garden with a mix of flowers, herbs, fruit and vegetables. Get here before opening time if possible; the house is immensely popular and tours are by timed ticket. Hill Top was never Beatrix Potter's permanent home, but some of the author's personal belongings can be seen in the house and you can buy Potter-themed gifts from the shop. For more about Beatrix Potter, see p 30. *Near Sawrey, Hawkshead.* ☎ *015394 36269. www.national trust.org.uk. Admission £6.20 adults; £3.10 children; £15.50 family. Open house mid-Feb–mid-Mar Sat–Thurs 11am–3.30pm; mid-Mar–Oct Sat–Thurs 10.30am–4.30pm; garden mid-Feb–Mar daily 11am–4pm; first 2 wks Mar and Nov–24th Dec daily 10am–4pm; mid-Mar–Oct daily 10.30am–5pm.*

② ★ St Michael's & All Angels Church. At the top of the hill behind Hawkshead Grammar School, this parish church was preceded by a Norse chapel in the 13th century. Parts of the walls date to the 14th century, but most of it is at least two centuries younger. It has a square bell tower at one end and its eight bells are one of the church's main attractions. Every Sunday they ring for half an hour before 9.30am service and Evensong at 5.30pm. *Main Street.* ☎ *015394 36301. www.hawksheadbenefice.co.uk Admission free. Open daily 9am–5pm.*

③ ★ Hawkshead Grammar School. Set back from the Main Street, this school was founded by the Archbishop of York in 1585. In its heyday it was regarded as one of the finest schools in the country, but today it is the Wordsworthian association that draws the crowds. He attended the school here for several years. His name is scratched into one

Beatrix Potter's former home at Hill Top Farm is just a couple of miles from Hawkshead.

Wordsworth went to school at Hawkshead Grammar.

of the desks, but there is no proof that Wordsworth himself was responsible. For more information on this and William Wordsworth, see p 34. *Hawkshead.* ☎ *015394 36735. www.hawksheadgrammar.org.uk. Admission £2. Open Apr–Oct Mon–Sat 10am–1pm and 2pm–5pm (Oct until 3.30pm); Sun 1pm–5pm; closed Nov–Mar.*

④ ★ Beatrix Potter Gallery.
This gallery is located in the former offices of Beatrix Potter's husband, the solicitor William Heelis. Now run by the National Trust, it contains manuscripts, sketches and paintings produced by Beatrix Potter for her animal stories. Part of the premises has been recreated as it was in Mr Heelis's time, complete with ledgers and old-fashioned files. *Main Street, Hawkshead.* ☎ *015394 36355. www.nationaltrust.org.uk. Admission £4.20 adults; £2.10 children; £10.50 family. Open mid-Feb–mid-Mar Sat–Thurs 11am–3.30pm; mid-Mar–Oct 10.30am–4.30pm.*

Where to **Stay & Dine**

Anne Tyson's House Wordsworth lodged here for a time while studying at Hawkshead Grammar School. The main house is now a self-catering cottage, but there's also simple but comfortable B&B accommodation available. *Wordsworth Street.* ☎ *015394 36405. www.anne tysons.co.uk. Doubles £58–£90; cottages £295–£540 per week. Maestro, MC, V.*

Buttercups Café INTERNATIONAL Come for a Buttercups English breakfast with sausage and egg, speciality teas, light bites like homemade soup and roll, or try the restaurant menu, which includes chicken curry, cannelloni and ratatouille. *Laburnum House, The Square.* ☎ *015394 36490. www. buttercupscafe.co.uk. Mains from £7.50. AE, Maestro, MC, V.*

The Croft Caravan Site A campsite in a sheltered fellside setting close to the village. You can pitch a tent or rent a furnished caravan. *North Lonsdale Road.* ☎ *015394 36374. www.hawkshead-croft.com. Tent/motorhome for 2 people and one vehicle £14.50–£17.25; touring caravan £17.50–£21.50; car £3–£4; extra adult £3.50; child £1–£1.25. Maestro, MC, V.*

Ivy House Hotel & Restaurant BRITISH This Grade II-listed house in the centre of Hawkshead has several very comfortable guestrooms (some with four-posters). The restaurant is open to non-residents for breakfast, lunch, afternoon tea and dinners of lamb shank, Gressingham duck and local trout. *Main Street.* ☎ *015394 36204. www.ivyhouse hotel.com. Doubles £100. Restaurant*

Ivy House Hotel & Restaurant is located in a Grade II-listed building.

open daily 8.30am-8pm. Mains from £13.50. Maestro, MC, V.

The King's Arms Hotel *EURO-PEAN* This is a 500-year-old inn with beams and open-log fires. The guestrooms have dark wood furnishings, some with four-poster beds, and there are also self-catering properties available to rent. The restaurant serves a mix of traditional Cumbrian dishes and continental favourites. *The Square.* ☎ *015394 36372. www. kingsarmshawkshead.co.uk. Doubles £74–£94; cottages from £320 per week. Restaurant open 12pm–8pm. Mains from £9.95. Maestro, MC, V.*

Poppi Red With its brightly painted exterior and an inviting terrace, this café-shop is understandably popular. Inside it's just as bright, serving cakes, coffee and wine in quirky ceramics. It sells gifts, clothes and a few curios. *Main Street.* ☎ *015394 36434. www. poppi-red.co.uk. Open daily 9am– 6pm. Maestro, MC, V.*

Queens Head Hotel *BRITISH* A handsome 17th-century building in Hawkshead village centre, offering spacious accommodation and a cosy bar/restaurant with roaring winter fires. Proud of its carefully sourced local produce, the restaurant serves inventive Cumbrian dishes: duck with raspberry vinaigrette and lamb with an orange demi-glaze. *Main Street.* ☎ *015394 36271 www.queenshead hotel.co.uk. Doubles £90–£110. Restaurant open 12pm–8pm. Mains from £13.95. Maestro, MC, V.*

Sun Cottage Café *EUROPEAN* Surrounded by pots of flowers, this tiny café has just a few seats inside, creating a warm and intimate atmosphere. You can just stop for cake or enjoy a full meal of ham hock terrine, Greek salad and topside beef filled with the chef's own-recipe stuffing. *Main Street.* ☎ *015394 36123. Mains from £5. Maestro, MC, V.*

Flowers frame the tiny Sun Cottage Café.

Kendal

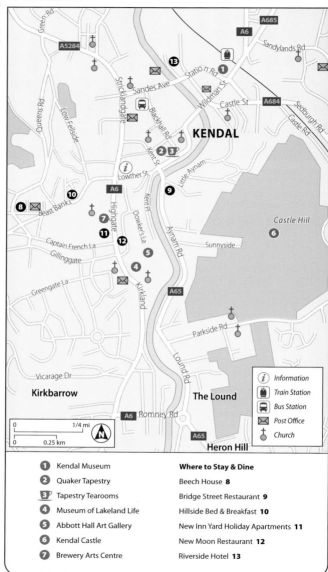

1 Kendal Museum

2 Quaker Tapestry

3 Tapestry Tearooms

4 Museum of Lakeland Life

5 Abbott Hall Art Gallery

6 Kendal Castle

7 Brewery Arts Centre

Where to Stay & Dine

Beech House **8**

Bridge Street Restaurant **9**

Hillside Bed & Breakfast **10**

New Inn Yard Holiday Apartments **11**

New Moon Restaurant **12**

Riverside Hotel **13**

Kendal is the first town most visitors encounter if they are travelling from the south by car, hence its much-used strapline 'Gateway to the Lakes'. The town dates back to the 8th century and has had a market charter since 1189. The town thrived on the wool industry, but today the old factory yards are filled with shops and restaurants. Kendal's main attractions include the Quaker Tapestry, Kendal Museum, the Museum of Lakeland Life and Abbot Hall art gallery. The parish church on Kirkland also deserves a look—its nave is one of the widest in the country, only a fraction narrower than York Minster. START: **Kendal Museum. Transport: train to Kendal; bus 552, 555, X1, X8, 45.**

1 ★ kids **Kendal Museum.** Kendal Museum was first opened in 1796 by William Todhunter to display his collection of **fossils, stuffed animals and curios.** Today its wide-ranging contents have something to interest most visitors. With the help of worksheets, children can discover more about prehistoric Cumbria, the Roman legacy and the story of 13th-century Kendal Castle. It's a **hands-on** museum: you don't need to be a child to try on a pair of Roman shoes, play a slate xylophone, do some fossil rubbing or follow a creepy crawly trail. *Station Road.* ☎ *01539 721374. www.kendal museum.org.uk, Admission £2.80 adults; £2.20 seniors; children and full-time students free. Open Thurs–Sat 12pm–5pm.*

Panel at The Quaker Tapestry.

The Museum of Lakeland Life takes you back in time.

2 ★ **Quaker Tapestry.** Inside the Friends Meeting House, this tapestry consists of 77 hand-embroidered panels celebrating the story of the Quaker movement. It is the product of thousands of painstaking hours given voluntarily by over 4,000 Quaker men and women from many countries. Each panel focuses on a specific aspect of Quaker history, starting with the founding Quaker **George Fox** and the humiliations suffered by early Quaker preacher and missionary Mary Fisher (1623–98) for her beliefs. There are sections devoted to their schools, marriage, trades and daily life.

I found the most touching ones were those relating to their role as pacifists and bearers during wartime, and their aid to the needy and sick around the world, especially to the Irish during the Great Famine. As I arrived, there was a buzz of excitement as the Quaker Tapestry had just won an industry award for best **Small Visitor Attraction of the Year.**

There's a shop here, occasional embroidery workshops where you can learn new techniques (see website for upcoming dates) and a tearoom next door (see below). *Friends Meeting House, Stramongate.*

☎ *01539 722975. www.quaker-tapestry.co.uk. Admission £6 adults; £5 concessions; £2 children; £12 family. Open Apr–Dec Mon–Fri 10am–5pm.*

Take a Break

3 **Tapestry Tearooms.** The tearooms are worth a visit even if you don't want to see the tapestry. Tables are tucked away into small rooms and nooks where you can munch on homemade quiche and salad or warming fresh soup, or try one of its tempting cakes. *Stramongate* ☎ *01539 722975. Open Mon–Fri 10am–4.30pm.*

4 ★ **Museum of Lakeland Life.** This excellent museum shares the same site as the **Abbott Hall Art Gallery** (see below). If you want to see the museum first, enter the car park via Peppercorn Lane off Kirkland. Multifarious contents evoke many scenes of **Lakeland life:** reconstructed workshops complete with artisans tools and instruments, rooms recreated in period styles. There are sections on the Arts and Crafts movement and the influence of John Ruskin; memorabilia owned

Kendal's Yards

The old yards off Stricklandgate once housed the town's industrial workshops. All kinds of trades took place, but the woollen industry predominated, and every stage of the process was carried out here: combing, dyeing, spinning, weaving and knitting. The textile trade attracted imports such as sugar and tobacco from the colonies to Kendal, kick-starting new manufacturing industries. One of these was snuff-making (now virtually obsolete); another was Kendal Mint Cake—still regarded as an essential emergency ration in any serious explorer's backpack since being taken on Shackleton's Antarctic expedition in 1922, and the first ascent of Everest. Today the tourist industry has breathed new economic life into several of these old yards, which are now buzzing with shops and cafés. Three of the liveliest are Elephant Yard (www.elephantyard.com), Blackhall Yard (www.blackhallyard.co.uk) and Wainwrights Yard (www.wainwrightsyard.com). The busy shopping street of Stricklandgate is home to the Westmorland Shopping Centre (www.westmorlandshopping.com) and www.farrerscoffee.co.uk.

by the author of *Swallows and Amazons* Arthur Ransome; you can walk through an 18th-century kitchen or an Edwardian street. *Kirkland.* ☎ *01539 722464. www.lakeland museum.org.uk. Admission £5.75 adults; £3.75 children/full-time students; £15 family.*

5 ★ **Abbott Hall Art Gallery.** Just across the courtyard from the Lakeland museum, Abbott Hall is a Grade I-listed Georgian mansion, built in 1759 by Colonel George Wilson. The local council bought the property in 1897 to use the grounds as a public park. The house fell into disrepair and, like Blackwell (see p 45), was rescued by the Lakeland Arts Trust. The property was restored and opened as an art gallery in 1962. Today it has an impressive collection of paintings, **watercolours, sculpture and decorative arts** from the 18th– 20th centuries. The watercolours seem particularly appropriate in

these high-ceilinged Georgian rooms. Highlights include Lake District landscapes by Constable, among others, and a collection of drawings by John Ruskin. The gallery hosts temporary exhibitions of 20th-century and contemporary works. There's a stylish café downstairs offering imaginative light bites, coffee and cakes. *Strickland.* ☎ *01539 722464. www.*

Abbott Hall is a fine Georgian House.

Brewery Arts Centre.

abbotthall.org.uk. *Admission £6.35 adults; free under 18yrs/full-time students under 25.*

6 ★ Kendal Castle There's not much left of this 13th-century castle but it has an interesting past. Built on a mound on the east side of the River Kent, it provided a tremendous vantage point over the town. For 200 years it was owned by the Parr family, and was the birthplace of Catherine Parr, the last and luckiest wife of Henry VIII (she was the only one to survive him). The castle fell into decline after the last baron died in the 15th century. Some of the walls and one of the towers survive, and the panoramic view is worth the climb, stretching as far as the Pennines in the distance. *Access from Sunnyside Parr Street (Ayman Road) or Castle Road. Admission free. Open 24-7.*

7 Brewery Arts Centre. The centre of Kendal's arts scene puts on a lively programme of cinema, music, theatre, dance, comedy and literature. It hosts festivals and youth events, plus a range of language, art and design workshops. It has several on-site eateries. *Highgate.* ☎ *01539 795090. www. breweryarts.co.uk.*

Where to **Stay & Dine**

Abbott Hall Coffee Shop

BRITISH Set away from the bustle of Kendal's central streets, this is a good place to stop for a coffee break or light lunch of soup and sandwiches. *Abbott Hall Art Gallery.* ☎ *01539 722464. www.abbotthall. org.uk. Sandwiches from £5.35. Maestro, MC, V.*

Beech House

This B&B has six contemporary, stylish rooms and parking space behind the house. Deluxe rooms have king-size beds, velvet sofas and views across the green. *40 Greenside.* ☎ *01539 720385. www.beechhouse-kendal. co.uk. Doubles £80–£90. Maestro, MC, V.*

Brewery Arts Centre

INTERNATIONAL There's a choice of eating places here: try the **Grain Store Restaurant** for fresh local produce and the **Intro Café Bar** for a child-friendly environment and a 'healthy choice' menu. The **Warehouse Café** is a favourite meeting place, a daytime café with WiFi access and an art house cinema at night. Finally, the **Vats Bar** is a cool hangout where you can enjoy drinks and pizza. *Highgate.* ☎ *01539 725133. www.breweryarts.co.uk. Open Grain Store daily 10am–2.30pm and 5.30pm–9pm; Intro Café Bar daily 9.30am–11pm; Warehouse Café daily 9am–6pm; Vats Bar Mon–Fri 11.30am–2.30pm and 5.30pm–11pm; Sat 11.30am–12am; Sun 11.30am–11pm. AE, Maestro, MC, V.*

The 1657 Chocolate House in Branthwaite Brow.

Bridge Street Restaurant

BRITISH Located in a Grade II-listed Georgian building, this simple, stylish restaurant has two first-floor dining rooms. The contemporary menu includes pan-fried seabass, Kentmere lamb and poached halibut. *1 Bridge Street.* ☎ *01539 738855. www.bridgestreetkendal.co.uk. Entrees from £13.75. AE, Maestro, MC, V.*

Hillside Bed & Breakfast

This is a small, homely B&B in a Victorian house just a few minutes' walk from Kendal town centre. Inside, the guest bedrooms are decorated simply with neutral tones and pine furniture. *4 Beast Banks.* ☎ *01539 722836. www.hillside-kendal.co.uk. Doubles £62–£78. AE, Maestro, MC, V.*

New Inn Yard Holiday Apartments

Not far from the Brewery Arts Centre, these seven self-catering apartments in a Victorian building have a stylish contemporary feel. Apartments cater for two to eight people, and all have kitchen facilities. *40 Greenside.* ☎ *01539 721275. www.kendalselfcatering. co.uk. Doubles £355–£435 per week, 4–8 person apt £410–£645 per week. Cheque or bank transfer.*

New Moon Restaurant

MODERN BRITISH This restaurant serves modern British cuisine for lunch and dinner. You can expect dishes such as grilled chicken with sweet potato mash, homemade lamb burger and grilled red mullet fillets. *129 Highgate.* ☎ *01539 729254. www.new moonrestaurant.co.uk. Entrees from £9.95. Maestro, MC, V.*

Riverside Hotel

This hotel on the banks of the River Kent has 47 attractive modern rooms, some with four-poster beds. There's also a restaurant and a leisure centre with a heated indoor pool. *Beezon Road, Stramongate Bridge.* ☎ *01539 734861. www.riversidekendal.co.uk. Doubles £88–£150. AE, Maestro, MC, V.*

Stop for refreshments at the Quaker Tearooms.

Keswick

1. Moot Hall
2. Keswick Museum
   & Art Gallery
3. Peddlar's Cafe
4. Cars of the Stars
5. James Bond Museum
6. Cumberland Pencil
   Museum
7. Theatre by the Lake
8. Keswick Launches
   & Derwentwater

Where to Stay & Dine

Bramblewood Cottage
  Guest House 9
Castlerigg Hall Caravan
  & Camping Park 10
The Cornish Pasty 11
Derwent Lodge Hotel 12
The George 13
Howe Keld 14
Kings Arms Hotel 15

Luca's Ristorante
  & Pizzeria 16
Old Keswickian 17
Queens Hotel 18
Sienna's Bar & Grill 19
Skiddaw Hotel 20

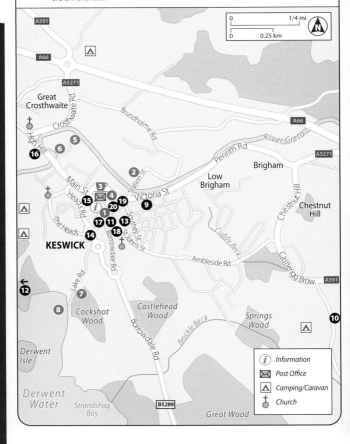

0		1/4 mi
0	0.25 km	

i Information
✉ Post Office
⛺ Camping/Caravan
† Church

Keswick is set in the northern Lake District on the banks of Derwentwater with Skiddaw rising to the north. The town grew in the 16th century on the back of local copper mining in nearby Borrowdale Valley, but there's evidence of a Neolithic settlement at Castlerigg Stone Circle. Graphite was also mined, the pencil industry reaching its peak in the 18th and 19th centuries. It was the association with the Romantic artists and poets, as well as the arrival of a train line in the 1860s, which attracted visitors. Today its lakeside setting and easy access to Skiddaw, Blencathra and other fells make it a popular base for outdoor enthusiasts. In town, there are several museums, outdoor gear shops, restaurants and accommodation.
START: **Moot Hall, Main Street. Transport: A66/A591; bus 555.**

❶ ★★★ **Moot Hall.** The Moot Hall is the most striking building on the pedestrianized Main Street. Built in 1813, this is a quaint grey-stone building with a tower at one end. It replaced an earlier 16th-century courthouse, and was used as the town hall. Look out for the one-handed clock and the arcaded ground floor, once used as market stalls. Today it houses one of the busiest tourist information centres in the Lake District and an art gallery upstairs. *Main Street.* ☎ *017687 72645. www.keswick.org. Open daily 9.30am–5.30pm.*

❷ ★ **Keswick Museum & Art Gallery.** This charming, rather old-fashioned museum reveals much about the life and history of the Lake District, with sections exploring its landscape, the beginnings of the National Trust and climbing on the fells. Its eclectic curiosities range from Napoleon's teacup to Britain's rarest fish. *Station Road.* ☎ *01768 773263. Admission free. Open Tues–Sat 10am–4pm. Closed winter 2009–Mar 2010 for refurbishment.*

The Moot Hall dominates Keswick's Main Street.

See vehicles from all your favourite TV series at Cars of the Stars.

Take a Break

3 Peddlar's Cafe. Enjoyable even for carnivores, this wholesome vegetarian fare is worth a try. Fill up on veggie nachos or lasagne, a range of daily specials, soup and sandwiches. Upstairs there's a bike shop where you can hire bicycles or buy spares. *Bell Close Car Park.* ☎ *017687 74492. Open Tues–Sun during museum hours.*

4 ★ Cars of the Stars. One of two Keswick museums owned and

conceived by local dentist Peter Nelson (see **5** below), Cars of the Stars will fascinate film and vehicle enthusiasts alike. The remarkable collection includes iconic vehicles familiar from films such as *Chitty Chitty Bang Bang, Batman, The Flintstones, Back to the Future* and *Mad Max.* There's also a selection of cars that featured in cult TV classics such as *Only Fools and Horses, Knightrider, The A Team* and *Thunderbirds.*

The gift shop sells celebrity-signed photos and model cars. *Standish Street.* ☎ *017687 72090. www.carsofthestars.com. Admission £5 adults; £3 children 3–15 yrs. Open Feb half-term holiday, Easter week–Dec daily 10am–5pm; Dec–Christmas weekends 10am–5pm.*

5 ★ James Bond Museum. This recently opened museum has hit the headlines. Owned and run by Peter Nelson of Cars of the Stars fame (see above), it contains an impressive line-up of vehicles seen in James Bond movies.

Prized pieces include the Aston Martin DB5 gadget car used in *Goldfinger,* the Lotus Esprit S1 from *The Spy Who Loved Me* and the Ford Mustang from *Diamonds Are Forever.*

The Cumberland Pencil Museum tells the story of Borrowdale slate.

Canon Rawnsley

Born in Oxfordshire in 1851, Canon Hardwicke Drummond Rawnsley was ordained after studying at Oxford and moved to the Lake District to become vicar of Crosthwaite Church, near Keswick, in 1877. He fell in love with the Lake District and spent the rest of his life trying to protect it. Together with Octavia Hill and Sir Robert Hunter, he set up the National Trust in 1895. His views influenced Beatrix Potter, who bought large areas of land in the Lake District and bequeathed it to the National Trust. Towards the end of his life, Rawnsley owned Allan Bank, a house in Grasmere once occupied by William Wordsworth for three years. When Rawnsley died in 1920, he left it to the National Trust.

You'll find lots of Bond memorabilia in the shop. *Carding Mill Lane.* ☎ *01768 774044. www.thebond museum.com. Admission £6 adults; £4 children. Open daily 10am–5pm.*

6 ★ kids **Cumberland Pencil Museum.** This absorbing museum traces the history of a long-established local industry dating from the discovery of black-lead (graphite) in the Borrowdale valley. It's an excellent attraction for children (see p 59), bringing the subject to life with a film and quiz. Don't miss the wartime pencils issued to RAF fighter pilots, containing a map of Germany and a compass in a secret compartment, or the World's Longest Pencil (7 feet long). Kids can try out the pencils in the sketchers' area. *Southey Works, Carding Mill Lane.* ☎ *017687 73626. www. pencilmuseum.co.uk. Admission £3.25 adults; £1.75 under 16 yrs and seniors; £2.50 students. Open daily 9.30am–5pm.*

7 ★ **Theatre by the Lake.** Few theatres anywhere have a better setting than this one overlooking Derwentwater. During the summer, it presents plays by visiting theatre companies and a mixed programme of dance, operetta and musicals,

music and exhibitions. It also hosts several festivals during the year, including literature, jazz, film and the outdoors.

Pre-theatre suppers are served in the Friends' Gallery (book ahead) or coffee and afternoon teas during the day. *Lakeside* ☎ *017687 74411. Theatrebythelake.co.uk. Bar open performance nights 10am–10pm, meals available in Friends' Gallery from 5pm but booking is essential.*

8 ★ **Keswick Launches & Derwentwater.** Lake cruisers make

A ride on a Keswick launch is a good way to see Derwentwater.

round trips of the lake, stopping at seven points where you can hop on and off at will or travel the full circle. Hawes End is a popular place to alight for the trek up Catbells (p 150) and its stunning views across the lake and fells. Or take a lakeshore walk through Brandlehow Woods, the National Trust's very first land acquisition in the Lake District. Stop

for refreshment at the Lodore Falls Hotel and visit the cascading waterfalls behind it. At Friar's Crag there's a memorial to John Ruskin. *Lakeshore.* ☎ *017687 72263. www. keswick-launch.co.uk. Admission £8.50 adults; £4.25 children; £20 family. Open summer approx 10am–6.15pm; winter 11.30am–4.15pm.*

Where to **Stay & Dine**

Bramblewood Cottage Guest House
A few minutes from the town centre, this stone-built B&B has five contemporary double en suite guestrooms and one twin, each with crisp, white sheets and contrasting cushions and throws. *2 Greta Street www.bramblewood keswick.com. Doubles £56–£72. AE, Maestro, MC, V.*

Castlerigg Hall Caravan & Camping Park
This site just outside Keswick has spectacular views and pitches for tents, motorhomes and caravans. There's also a restaurant, shop and launderette on-site. *Nr Castlerigg.* ☎ *017687 74499. www.castlerigg.co.uk. Caravan/ motorhome (and 2 people) £16.50–£20; additional person £2.50–£2.75; camping adult £5.50–£6.75; child £2.50–£3.30. Maestro, MC, V.*

The Cornish Pasty
BRITISH For lunch on the hop, The Cornish Pasty is a good stop. The smell of pasties hot from the oven is hard to resist. *3 Lake Road* ☎ *017687 772205. Open Mon–Sat 9am–5pm. Pasties from £2.50. Maestro, MC, V.*

Derwent Lodge Hotel
On the north-west side of Derwentwater, this small Georgian hotel has eight classical guestrooms and views of Skiddaw, Catbells and the lake. You can enjoy home-cooking in the

restaurant and relax in the lounge bar here. *Portinscale* ☎ *017687 73145 www.derwentlodgehotel. co.uk. Doubles £78–£180. AE, Maestro, MC, V.*

The George
BRITISH You'll find good pub grub at this town-centre pub. Keswick's oldest coaching inn, it has a menu of slow-cooked lamb, steaks, seabass and Cumberland roast ham. There are 13 traditional guestrooms upstairs. *St John's Street.* ☎ *017687 72076. www. georgehotelkeswick.co.uk. Restaurant open daily 5.30pm–9pm (Fri and Sat 9.30pm). Mains from £7.95. AE, Maestro, MC, V.*

Howe Keld
This recently refurbished property is now a modern B&B in central Keswick. They adhere to an environmental policy to minimize waste and conserve energy. *5–7 The Heads.* ☎ *017687 72417 www.howekeld.co.uk. Doubles £70–£120. Maestro, MC, V.*

Kings Arms Hotel
A former coaching inn dating back to the 17th century, the Kings Arms combines both traditional and contemporary furnishings in the bedrooms. Downstairs the restaurant menu remains fresh, local and homemade. *Main Street* ☎ *017687 72083. www.kings armskeswick.co.uk. Doubles £88–£120. Maestro, MC, V.*

Ye Olde Friars is a sweetshop fantasy.

Luca's Ristorante & Pizzeria

ITALIAN Luca's prepares fresh Italian food and much of it is even gluten-free. Tuck into tuna steaks marinated in basil, vegetarian risotto, bruschetta or a range of pizza and pasta. *High Hill.* ☎ *017687 74621. www.lucasristorante.co.uk. Open Tues–Fri (and Sun if bank holiday on Mon) 6pm–9pm; Sat 5pm–9.30pm. Mains from £9. Maestro, MC, V.*

Old Keswickian

BRITISH For cheap eats and fast food, this eat-in or take-away fish-and-chip shop is a relaxed choice. You can also get fishcakes, homemade pies and veggie burgers. *Market Square.* ☎ *017687 73861. www.oldkeswickian.co.uk. Open daily 11am–11.30pm (eat-in until 9.30pm). Mains from £4.50. Maestro, MC, V.*

Queens Hotel

This central Keswick hotel has 35 en suite rooms of different styles, some with four-poster beds and views of the fells. There's also undercover, off-street parking. *Main Street* ☎ *017687 73333 www.queenshotel.co.uk. Doubles £60–£140. AE, Maestro, MC, V.*

Sienna's Bar & Grill

BRITISH Brightly coloured, trendy furnishings and a menu to match make this restaurant a good choice for either drinks or dinner. Expect steaks and salad on the menu and cocktails until late. *21 Station Street.* ☎ *017687 80430. www.siennasbarandgrill.com. Open daily 5.30pm–9pm (9.30pm Sat–Sun); bar daily 12pm–11pm (12am Wed–Sat). Mains from £8.95.*

Skiddaw Hotel

MODERN BRITISH This central Keswick hotel is right on the Main Street and has 43 contemporary guestrooms. There's also a lounge bar and a restaurant, 31 The Square, which serves dishes such as fresh Borrowdale trout, salmon fishcakes and ribeye steaks. *Main Street.* ☎ *017687 772071. www.lakedistricthotels.net. Doubles £136–£176.*

Penrith

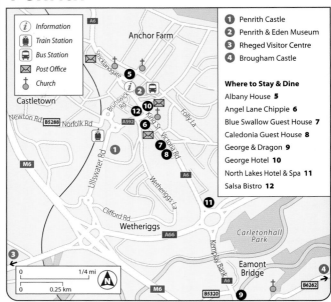

(i)	Information
🚉	Train Station
🚌	Bus Station
✉	Post Office
✝	Church

❶ Penrith Castle
❷ Penrith & Eden Museum
❸ Rheged Visitor Centre
❹ Brougham Castle

Where to Stay & Dine

Albany House **5**
Angel Lane Chippie **6**
Blue Swallow Guest House **7**
Caledonia Guest House **8**
George & Dragon **9**
George Hotel **10**
North Lakes Hotel & Spa **11**
Salsa Bistro **12**

Penrith is located on the edge of the lush, green Eden Valley, set between the Lake District fells and the North Pennines. Its position made it an important trade route with the Romans and a flashpoint for skirmishes between the Scots and English in the 13th century. Today it remains an important shopping hub, a lively market town with red sandstone buildings, independent and specialist stores. Just outside the town are several attractions, including Brougham Castle and Rheged. With good transport links, it's a good base for exploring the East Lakes and the Eden Valley. START: **Penrith Castle. Transport: train to Penrith; bus X4, X5, 104, 106, 108.**

❶ ★ **Penrith Castle.** This 14th–15th-century castle was built to defend northern England from the Scots. In the 1470s, Richard III, then Duke of Gloucester, turned it into a luxury home. Little remains of this opulence, but the castle walls are still more or less intact. *Opposite Penrith station www. english-heritage.org.uk. Admission* *free. Open summer daily 7.30am– 9pm; winter daily 9.30am–4.30pm.*

❷ ★ **Penrith & Eden Museum.** Until the 1970s, this building had been home to Robinsons School for 300 years. It was named after the wealthy local merchant and benefactor William Robinson, who had made his money in London. There's a wide-ranging collection here; you

See the impressive ruins at Penrith Castle.

can expect dinosaur footprints, Roman coins, several landscape paintings, local photographs and curiosities belonging to Penrith personalities such as Percy Toplis, the 'Monocled Mutineer'.

The local tourist information centre is also based here, so you can pick up more local information as you visit. *Robinson School, Middlegate. Admission free. Open Mon–Sat 10am–5pm; Sun Apr–Oct 1pm–4.45pm.*

❸ ★ Rheged Visitor Centre.
This popular family attraction built into a hillside just off the M6 (p 49, bullet ❸) has lots of shopping and leisure facilities under its startling turf-covered roof. Named after a British-Celtic kingdom that existed in the Dark Ages, Rheged is an all-weather discovery centre with a six-storey cinema screen showing 3D films suitable for children. Retail outlets sell local produce and crafts in the indoor mall. There's an outdoor play park and indoor crafts, and exhibitions telling you more about the ancient kingdom of Rheged and local Cumbrian history. *Junction of A66 and A592. ☎ 01768 868000. www.rheged.com. Admission giant movies £4.95 adults; £3.95 concessions; £3 children 5–15 yrs; £14 family (2 adults and 3 children); outdoor*

play £1.50 per child; indoor soft play free–£2.50 per hour under 6mths–over 1 yr. Create £3.50–£6.95 per item.

❹ ★ Brougham Castle. Just 1.5 miles outside Penrith, this castle was built in the 13th century by Robert de Vieuxpont, an agent of King John I, as a barrier against the Scots. It stands on the site of a Roman fortress, beside the River Eamont. Today it's a majestic ruin in the care of English Heritage. The original gatehouse and a later tower

Penrith is a bustling market town.

Shopping in Penrith

Penrith is known for its independent specialist shops, harking back to an era before the depressing cloning of Britain's high streets with identical chain stores. At the top of my list are **Cranstons Butchers**, www.cranstons.net (p 49, ❷), which makes giant Cumberland sausages, **The Toffee Shop**, www.thetoffeeshop.co.uk, which sells mouth-watering handmade fudge, and **The Gem Den**, an Aladdin's Cave of gemstones, jewellery and fossils. At the **Beacon Bakery** you'll be drawn in by the aroma of fresh homemade bread, cakes and scones, and **Market Place News & Gifts** sells the kinds of sweets in jars from a generation ago. There are haberdashers, cobblers, small shops selling rosewood furniture, yarn, leather goods and jewellery and gifts. Most are clustered along King Street, through Middlegate, or tucked off narrow Angel Lane, Corn Market, Little Dockray and Devonshire Arcade.

survive. The redoubtable Lady Anne Clifford was the last to occupy the castle in the 17th century, and though she undertook some restoration, when she died in 1676 it fell into disrepair. *Off the A66 (first turning right after the 2nd Penrith roundabout if coming from Kendal). www.english-heritage.org.uk. Admission £3.50 adults; £1.80 children; £3 concessions. Open Apr–Sep daily 10am–5pm.*

Where to **Stay & Dine**

Albany House This Victorian house has comfortable contemporary rooms, including a family room, and is within easy walking distance of the town centre. *5 Portland Place* ☎ *01768 863072 www.albany-house.org.uk. Doubles from £50. Maestro, MC, V.*

Angel Lane Chippie *BRITISH* A hole-in-the-wall chip shop (and Penrith's oldest), where you can nip in for a Friday-night fish supper and sizzling chips covered in salt and vinegar. *17 Angel Lane.* ☎ *01768 866762. Open 12pm–11pm. Fish and chips £3.50. Cash only.*

Blue Swallow Guest House Another of Penrith's Victorian B&Bs, this property has secure parking for bicycles. The rooms are traditional with comfortable divan beds. *11 Victoria Road* ☎ *01768 866335 www.blueswallow.co.uk. Doubles £60–£80. Maestro, MC, V.*

Caledonia Guest House. This central B&B has modern rooms with modern furnishings, feature wallpaper and complementing textiles. There's a mixture of family, twin and double rooms to choose from. *8 Victoria Road* ☎ *01768 864482 www.caledoniaguesthouse.co.uk. Doubles £60–£66. Cash or cheques only.*

Enjoy a spicy night at Mexican eatery Salsa.

George & Dragon *MODERN BRITISH* The produce used here mostly comes from the Lowther Estates, and the emphasis is on fresh and seasonal. The restaurant has an informal gastro-pub feel, and the changing menu includes dishes like wild garlic, spring vegetable and blue cheese risotto, confit of duck leg and shorthorn beef burger. Children's menus are also available. *Clifton, nr Penrith.* ☎ *01768 865381. Open lunch 12pm–2.30pm; afternoon tea 3pm–6pm; dinner 6pm–9.30pm. Mains from £9.50. Maestro, MC, V.*

George Hotel *MODERN BRITISH* This is a 300-year-old property with rooms in neutral tones with contrasting bedding. Downstairs there's a modern English restaurant and two bars. The relaxing restaurant serves traditional dishes with a fresh twist, such as Cumberland beer-battered haddock and roast red Cumberland Middlethwaite pork with roasted vegetables. *Devonshire Street.* ☎ *01768 862696. www. georgehotelpenrith.co.uk Doubles from £112. AE, Maestro, MC, V.*

North Lakes Hotel & Spa *BRITISH & EUROPEAN* This is a modern hotel and spa with a restaurant, bar and café and a heated indoor pool and gym. The restaurant works with local suppliers to produce a fresh seasonal menu of British and European dishes. *Ullswater Road.* ☎ *01768 868111. www.northlakes hotel.com. Doubles £112–£160. Restaurant open lunch 12.30pm–2pm (provided no conferences); dinner 7pm–9.15pm. Mains from £15.50. AE, Maestro, MC, V.*

Salsa Bistro *MEXICAN* A popular eatery in the heart of Penrith, Salsa Bistro serves sizzling fajitas and steaks on the grill, as well as Mexican-style tapas snacks and starters like chorizo nachos and stuffed jalapeno chilies. *1 New Keswick Street.* ☎ *01768 868666. Open daily 5.30pm–9.30pm. Maestro, MC, V.*

Ulverston

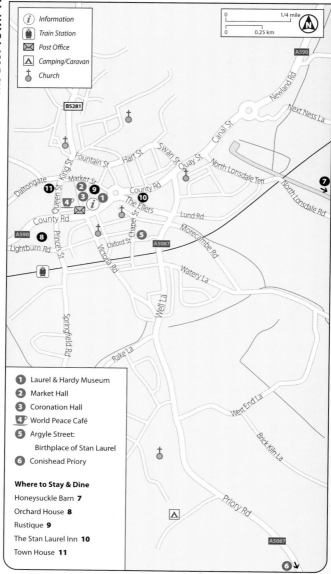

i Information

🚂 Train Station

✉ Post Office

△ Camping/Caravan

✝ Church

0 ——— 1/4 mile
0 ——— 0.25 km

1 Laurel & Hardy Museum

2 Market Hall

3 Coronation Hall

4 World Peace Café

5 Argyle Street:
   Birthplace of Stan Laurel

6 Conishead Priory

Where to Stay & Dine

Honeysuckle Barn **7**

Orchard House **8**

Rustique **9**

The Stan Laurel Inn **10**

Town House **11**

As you walk along the cobbled streets and narrow lanes of Ulverston, you can feel the sea breeze drifting in from Morecambe Bay. It's worth visiting just for the Laurel and Hardy Museum, but Ulverston's varied list of festivals or Conishead Priory's contemplative Buddhist retreats also attract many visitors. START: Laurel and Hardy Museum. Transport: car: A590; bus: 10, 11, X35, 60, 70, 511, 618; train: Ulverston station.

❶ ★★★ Laurel & Hardy Museum. I first visited this museum in its original home on Upper Brook Street, where manager Alan had been working and entertaining visitors with anecdotes about Laurel and Hardy for more than 30 years.

Inside was a cornucopia of memorabilia from the comedy legends, from life-size models and props to photos and letters written to fans by Stan; he wrote 25 a day according to Alan.

The collection was first put together by Bill Cubin in 1983, a lifelong fan, whose private collection had become too large and popular to keep hidden away. Bill died in 1997, but his daughter Marianne has kept his legacy alive.

Now the museum has a new home, with information boards guiding you round the collection of newspaper clippings and memorabilia, and a cinema where you can enjoy some classic Laurel and Hardy films, including *The Music Box*, for which they won an Academy Award. But do look out for Alan, who will remain part of the museum as long as he can. *Roxy Museum, Brogden Street. ☎ 01229 582292. www. laurel-and-hardy.co.uk. Admission £4 adults; £3 children under 12 yrs, seniors and students; £8 families. Open: daily 10am-5pm; closed Jan.*

❷ ★ Market Hall. Ulverston has had a street market since it received its market charter in 1280. But the market hall itself was built in the

The Laurel and Hardy Museum has the largest collection of memoralia by the comedy pair in the world.

Stan Laurel

Arthur Stanley Jefferson was born on 16th June, 1890 in Ulverston. Both his parents worked in the theatre, and he lived in his grandparents' terraced house in Argyle Street. He later moved to North Shields with his parents and then Glasgow, where he first stepped on the stage. He joined a travelling theatre group, playing Charlie Chaplin's understudy, and travelled to the United States. Here he began to write his own gags, and changed his name to Laurel. His first film with Oliver Hardy was *Duck Soup* in 1927; they went on to make more than 100 films together. Stan was devastated by the death of Hardy in 1957 and decided never to act again. During his long and successful career, he was involved in over 200 films. Stan died in 1965 following a heart attack.

19th century in an Italian style. You'll see locals here most days buying fresh produce, budget clothes and jewellery. Stroll through here from Brogden Street to Market Street, where there's still an outdoor market every Thursday and Saturday. *New Market Street. http:// ulverstonmarket.co.uk. Open: Mon, Tues, Thurs and Fri 9am–5pm.*

3 ★ Coronation Hall. This Ulverston landmark is known affectionately as The Coro by the locals. You can't miss it as it dominates the street, a large, early 20th-century building with a balcony at its centre. Stan Laurel waved from here at the thousands of fans who came to greet him on his last visit here in 1947—look out for the new statue of both Laurel and Hardy with the little dog Laughing Gravy outside the hall, unveiled by funny man Ken Dodd in April 2009.

You can stop for a few minutes' comtemplation at Conishead Priory.

Conishead Priory run residential Buddhist retreats.

The hall was built in 1913 with an English Renaissance-style interior, the frescoes of the Empire and cherubs have been painstakingly restored in heritage colours, along with the geometrical designs along its columns—see if you can spot the famous mouse among the ceiling carvings. While some find the classical pastiche a little gaudy, it represents an artistic penchant of the time. It's also the largest venue in South Cumbria, hosting a varied programme of theatre, music, dance and comedy. *County Square.* ☎ *01229 588944.*

Take a Break

4 **World Peace Café.** This café is a welcome stop-off for refreshment with a soft sofa by the window which you can sink into with a cappuccino or enjoy falafels, hummus and salads from the whole-food menu. *5 Cavendish Street.* ☎ *01229 587793. Mains from £4.50. AE, DC, MC, V. Lunch and dinner daily. Closed public hols.*

5 ★ **Argyle Street: Birthplace of Stan Laurel.** Laurel and Hardy fans won't want to come to

Festival Fun

Keep Ulverston's busy festival schedule in mind when you're booking your accommodation. The season gets going in February with the World Market Literary Festival Week, followed by the South Cumbria Music Festival in February. After that there are at least four events each month, including the Walking Festival and Spring Fun Fair in April; Spring Buddhist Festival and Cartmel Races in May; Ulverston Carnival in July; CAMRA Beer Festival in September; and a Dickensian Christmas Festival in November, when the lights are switched on. There are also food fairs every month, speciality markets in the summer and a Christmas food fair.

Look out for the Eddystone Lighthouse as you drive out of Ulverston.

Ulverston without visiting Stan's birthplace. One of a street of small terraced houses, there's a blue

plaque outside no. 3. The house is now privately occupied and not open to the public. *3 Argyle Street.*

⑥ ★ Conishead Priory. The grounds of this grand 19th-century house are a calming place to escape traditional sightseeing for a while. Just outside Ulverston, the house stands on the site of a priory dating back to the 12th century. During its long history, Conishead Priory has served variously as a hydropathic hotel, convalescence home for miners and a military hospital. Today it's a Buddhist centre—unheralded visitors are welcome to enjoy the gardens at any time of the year and pay a respectful visit to the modern temple. I found it a peaceful place to recharge spiritual batteries, and the Buddhists are happy to answer any questions you may have. *Priory Road.* ☎ *01229 584029. www. conisheadpriory.org.*

Where to **Stay & Dine**

Stan Laurel's birthplace is marked by a plaque.

Honeysuckle Barn This traditional B&B is a few minutes' drive out of Ulverston, just where the canal spills through the sea lock into Morecambe Bay. On sunny mornings you can enjoy breakfast outdoors overlooking the water. *Canal Foot.* ☎ *01229 585089. www.honey sucklebarn.net. Doubles £52–£70.*

Orchard House In a quiet part of town, this homely B&B places an emphasis on comfort. Framed by hanging baskets, which are in full bloom throughout the summer, there's a choice of immaculate twin, double and family rooms. *2 Hazelcroft Gardens.* ☎ *01229 586771. www.orchardhouseulverston.co.uk. Doubles from £65.*

The World Peace Café is run by buddhists from Conishead Priory.

Rustique *BRITISH & EUROPEAN*
This 40-seater restaurant offers
good-value meal deals and an a la
carte dinner menu. Lunch on duck
confit cake, mussels or pork belly,
and dine on braised ham hock,
grilled mackerel or seared confit of
duck. *Brogden Street.* ☎ *01229
587373. www.eatatrustique.co.uk.
Open deli Mon-Sat 9.30am-4pm
(Weds until 1pm); evening restaurant
Tue-Sat 7pm-9pm. Mains from £6.50;
menus from £15.50.*

The Stan Laurel Inn *BRITISH*
Named after Ulverston's local hero,
this pub has budget accommodation
that's bright, clean and central.
There's a modern pub menu here
too. *31 The Ellers.* ☎ *01229 582814.
www.thestanlaurel.co.uk. Doubles
from £60. Restaurant open 12pm–
9pm (food). Mains from £8.95.*

Town House A traditional B&B set
in a period Georgian property in the
town centre with en suite rooms for
up to three people. Breakfast can
include haddock, eggs benedict or
muffins. *16 Queen Street.* ☎ *01229
580172. www.townhouseulverston.
co.uk. Doubles £60.*

World Peace Café *VEGETARIAN*
Good wholesome organic food with
some creativity is the order of the
day at this café. Run by the Buddhists from Conishead Priory, the
café includes vegetarian dishes like
ricotta-stuffed courgette and stir-
fried Japanese noodles. There are
healthy options for kids. *5 Cavendish
Street.* ☎ *01229 587793. Mains
from £4.50. AE, DC, MC, V. Lunch
and dinner daily. Closed public hols.*

Whitehaven

1 The Rum Story
2 Quick Quest
3 The Harbour
4 The Beacon
5 Haig Colliery
   Mining Museum

Where to Stay & Dine

Glenfield Guest House 6
Lowther House 7
Moresby Hall 8
Tivoli Guest House 9
Wellington Bistro 10

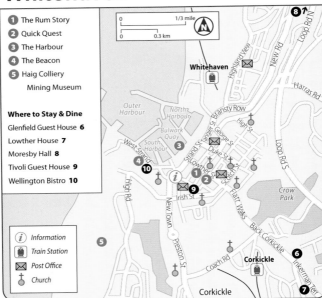

(i) Information
🚉 Train Station
✉ Post Office
† Church

Whitehaven was once one of the most important sea-
ports on the west coast of England, exporting coal and
importing rum, tobacco and slaves. The town's fortunes waned as
larger ports grew up, but the fine Georgian town planned mostly by
the powerful Lowther family remains. The harbour has received a
makeover, and The Beacon and the Rum Story give a fun, hands-on
insight into the town. START: **The Beacon. Transport: train to Whitehaven; bus X4, X5, 30, 46, 300, 301.**

1 ★★ kids **The Rum Story.** This
intriguing and rather unusual
museum takes you to exotic places
while revealing the gruesome role
of slavery in Jefferson's rum industry. You're accompanied by sounds
and stories as you walk from room
to room, each depicting life-sized
characters on Antiguan plantations
and slave ships, and the high life of
those who reaped the rewards.

After your complimentary tot of
rum, you can buy a bottle to take

home. On your way out, take a peek
into the administrative rooms,
which doubled as Mr Healis's office
in the 2006 film, *Miss Potter*. *27
Lowther Street.* ☎ *01946 592933.
www.rumstory.co.uk. Admission
£5.45 adults; £3.45 children under
16 yrs; £4.45 concessions. Open
daily 10am–4.30pm.*

2 ★ **Quick Quest.** Pick up a
Quick Quest map from The Rum
Story or the tourist information

centre on Market Place. This is a quiz with a map, guiding you around the town centre and introducing you to some of its important personalities, including John Paul Jones, who attacked the town during the American War of Independence. But I don't want to give you all the answers. It's an interesting tour, passing the harbour, the Georgian architecture and St Nicholas's Church. Also look out for the Whitehaven Labyrinth mosaic in the grounds of the former Trinity Church on Scotch Street, designed by Shaun Williamson as a Millennium project. *Whitehaven. Admission free.*

③ ★ **The Harbour.** Stroll along the Millennium Promenade to the marina, between Bulwark Quay and Lime Tongue; at night it's illuminated by a wave of light. Look out for the Miners' Memorial Statue, a moving tribute to the hard labour of people who contributed to the town's industrial heritage. Beyond is the Old Quay, dating back to 1633. *The Harbour.* ☎ *01946 692435. www.whitehaven-harbour.co.uk.*

Learn about the rise and fall of Whitehaven's maritime trade at The Rum Story.

Whitehaven's harbour has received a makeover.

④ ★★ **The Beacon.** Set beside Whitehaven's harbour, this round building really is a landmark. This interactive museum is a favourite with school groups, with much to interest children. Spanning five floors, the museum covers local art, photography, social history, archaeology, maps and lots more. There are life-sized models, period houses and parts of boats. Sound effects add to the intrigue with plenty of buttons and handles to press and pull. The basement café has harbour views. *West Strand.* ☎ *01946 592302. www.thebeacon-whitehaven. co.uk. Admission £5 adults; £4 concessions; under 16 yrs free with adult. Open Tues–Sun and bank holiday Mons 10am–4.30pm.*

⑤ ★ **Haig Colliery Mining Museum.** This museum is situated on the cliffs overlooking Whitehaven and stands at the site of the former Haig pit. This was Cumbria's last deep coal mine, closing in 1986, but was bought for £1 and converted into the present museum, run by volunteers. Coal-mining in Whitehaven was instigated in the 13th century by monks from St Bee's Abbey.

Visit the pit yard and cellar work-shop, and have a look at the displays depicting the town's long mining history. There are daily demonstrations of two fully restored winding engines. *Solway Road.*

☎ *01946 599949. www.haigpit. com. Admission free. Open daily 9.30am–4.30pm. Tours available. Bus 01 from Preston Street bus station.*

Where to **Stay & Dine**

Glenfield Guest House *MODERN BRITISH* The six guestrooms in this B&B are individually styled in traditional décor and retain the original Victorian fireplaces. *Back Corkickle.* ☎ *01946 691911. www. glenfield-whitehaven.co.uk. Doubles from £60.*

Lowther House This Victorian property has been transformed into a small boutique hotel in the heart of Whitehaven. The three carefully detailed guestrooms have crisp white sheets and fish-themed tiles in the en suite bathroom. *13 Inkerman Terrace.* ☎ *01946 63169. www. lowtherhouse-whitehaven.com. Doubles from £70.*

Moresby Hall A Grade I-listed historic house dating back to around 1620, this property is just two miles from Whitehaven. The spacious guestrooms are dressed impeccably with classical furnishings, two with four-poster beds. In addition, there are two converted farmhouse cottages, sleeping four and six people each. There's a walled garden in the grounds and a restaurant inside the house. *Moresby.* ☎ *01946 694385. www.moresbyhall.co.uk. Doubles £120–£150; cottages £315–£560 pw.*

Tivoli Guest House A small family-run guesthouse in the centre of Whitehaven, this is a popular choice with cyclists and walkers on the Coast-to-Coast route (p 152). There are double, twin and single rooms available. *156 Queen Street.*

☎ *01946 67400. www.barton88. plus.com. Doubles from £55.*

Wellington Bistro *BRITISH & EUROPEAN* On the ground floor of The Beacon museum, this café has picture windows looking onto the harbour. At lunch, food is fast and casual with homemade soup, jacket potatoes and sandwiches on the menu. In the evenings, the menu is more extensive with lamb shank, beef Wellington and aubergine parmagiana, as well as a selection of starters. You're advised to book in the evenings. *West Strand.* ☎ *01946 590231. www.thebeacon-whitehaven.co.uk. Open Tues, Wed and Sun 9.30am–4pm; Thurs–Sat 9.30am–9.30pm. Mains from £8.50. Maestro, MC, V.* ●

Statues in Whitehaven town centre.

Best Walking

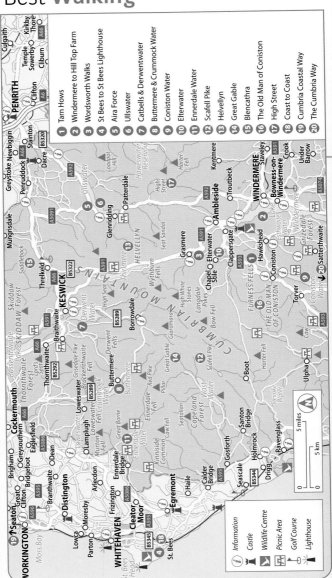

1. Tarn Hows
2. Windermere to Hill Top Farm
3. Wordsworth Walks
4. St Bees to St Bees Lighthouse
5. Aira Force
6. Ullswater
7. Catbells & Derwentwater
8. Buttermere & Crummock Water
9. Coniston Water
10. Elterwater
11. Ennerdale Water
12. Scafell Pike
13. Helvellyn
14. Great Gable
15. Blencathra
16. The Old Man of Coniston
17. High Street
18. Coast to Coast
19. Cumbria Coastal Way
20. The Cumbria Way

Information
Castle
Wildlife Centre
Picnic Area
Golf Course
Lighthouse

With breathtaking natural beauty that inspired Alfred Wainwright to painstakingly illustrate dozens of routes, it comes as no surprise that walking is the Lake District's most popular pursuit. Its 2225 miles of public footpaths include walks for all levels of fitness and some that are wheelchair accessible. The suggestions below are not a step-by-step guide, but an overview of some classic walks. Choose from short strolls to multi-day routes, or clamber up a high peak, where the boundaries blur between walking and scrambling. You might see fell runners dashing past, but set your own pace, follow the advice given in our Strategies chapter and keep to the waymarked trails to avoid erosion. You'll find all the equipment, clothing and maps you'll need in the Lake District's array of outdoor shops, particularly prevalent in Ambleside and Keswick.

Easy Walks

1 ★ Tarn Hows. One of the Lake District's most popular beauty spots, Tarn Hows is surrounded by conifers that are mirrored in the water. Formerly three smaller tarns, they merged into one in the 19th century when a dam was built. The gentle path around the shoreline is 1.5 miles long and wheelchair accessible, passing through woodland with delightful views of the fells beyond. *Near Hawkshead. 1.5 miles.*

2 ★ Windermere to Hill Top Farm. From Bowness, you can catch a boat across to the Ferry House on the west side of the lake. From here you can follow a combination of paths and quiet roads to Beatrix Potter's house, Hill Top. If you're feeling energetic you can walk around Esthwaite Water to Hawkshead and catch the bus back. *Near Sawrey. 2–7 miles.*

3 ★ Wordsworth Walks. These walks start in the centre of Grasmere and follow in the great man's footsteps around Grasmere and Rydal, noting his favourite haunts around the lakes, and including

There are pathways around Tarn Hows.

Explore Wordsworth's favourite places around Grasmere.

visits to Dove Cottage and the Wordsworth Museum. You can pick up a Literary Walks leaflet from the tourist office. *Grasmere. 1.7 miles.*

④ ★ St Bees to St Bees Lighthouse. From the beach in St Bees, follow the cliff-top path to St Bees Head for fantastic coastal views, a lighthouse and a nature reserve. This path forms part of the Cumbria Coastal Way (see p 153). *St Bees. 4 miles.*

⑤ ★ Aira Force. This National Trust waterfall beside Ullswater is surrounded by a network of woodland paths leading above and below the waterfall. *Ullswater 1 mile.*

Even small kids can manage a walk to Aira Force.

Lake Walks

⑥ ★ Ullswater. Starting from Glenridding, walk anti-clockwise around the lake to Howtown or Pooley Bridge and return to Glenridding on the steamer. The route starts on the road to Patterdale, turning left across Grizedale Beck and then left onto a woodland path that offers views over Ullswater. You can catch the ferry from Howtown Pier or continue along the lake's east bank. About a mile before Pooley Bridge, you'll pass through a campsite and back along the waterfront *Glenridding to Howtown/Pooley Bridge, 7–9 miles.*

⑦ ★ Catbells & Derwentwater. Possibly the most popular walk in the Lake District, this route takes you through a combination of lake and hill scenery. Most people start from Hawes End; you can take a ferry across from Keswick or drive round, but parking is tight. From here a path leads up Skelgill Bank and then Catbells, with unbeatable views of Derwentwater, Castlerigg Fell and Blencathra, and in the other direction towards the Derwent Fells. You can come back the way you came or descend down to Abbotts Bay and through the woods to Low Brandlehow. *Hawes End—Catbells—Low Brandlehow 3.5–4 miles.*

8 ★ Buttermere & Crummock Water. You can park at Gatesgarth or Buttermere village but arrive early in peak season and weekends to find a space. An easy track leads most of the way around Buttermere, except a short distance at the south-east end of the lake, when you'll have to walk (carefully) along ½ mile of road. There are a couple of places to park at the north end of Crummock Water and a path along the west side of the lake; half way along is the Lake District's highest waterfall, Scale Force, set in a wooded gorge. For a longer walk, you can continue uphill to Red Pike and High Stile, descending via Sour Milk Gill to Buttermere. *Buttermere 5 miles; Crummock Water 6-7 miles.*

9 ★ Coniston Water. The west side of Coniston Water is best for walking and includes a section of the Cumbria Way (see p 153). Just south of Coniston village, the path leads close to the water's edge, passing through Torver Wood Common, and continuing to the A5084. A mile along the road, you reach the Torver ferry terminal (summer service), otherwise return from Torver by bus or walk back. *Coniston Water. Flexible 1-7 miles.*

10 ★ Elterwater. There are several rivers, becks, tarns and waterfalls around Elterwater, making for a watery walk untaxing enough for young or novice walkers with marvellous views of the Langdale Pikes. There's a car park at Elterwater village, and from here you can walk east along a stretch of the Cumbria Way (p 153). It takes you around the north side of Elterwater and along the woodland river path to Skelwith Bridge and Skelwith Force (a small waterfall). The path continues westwards through fields and woodland to Colwith Force and Little Langdale Tarn before winding north back to

You can walk around Ullswater and take the steamer back.

Elterwater. *Elterwater 4.5–5 miles. 2–3 hours.*

11 ★ Ennerdale Water. One of the most remote lakes, Ennerdale Water has two beautiful walks along forest and lakeside paths. Park on the north side and follow the path through Bowness Knott Forest with the lake to your right. The path takes you beyond the east end of the lake alongside a river, which you cross to return along the south side of the lake. *Ennerdale Water 6.5-7 miles.*

Fell Walks

12 ★ Scafell Pike. England's highest peak (978 m/3209 ft) can be tackled from various starting points but the most popular starts at Wasdale Head at the northern end of Wastwater. Head through the campsite and up a long step-like path uphill beside a stream. Eventually the path splits; to the left is a winding path; the right-hand route is shorter but has a small scramble to tackle. Longer walks can include Scafell (England's second-highest mountain, 964 m/3163 ft) to the south.

13 ★ Helvellyn. England's third-highest peak (950 m/3117 ft) is most famous for its ridge, Striding Edge, a

The moody skies loom over Elterwater.

formidable knife-edge ridge. If you're not confident enough to tackle it, start from the Highpark Wood car park beside Thirlmere; from here there's a direct path up and down Helvellyn. For those that want to brave the ridge, enjoy the long but picturesque walk in from Glenridding via Gillside and onto Striding Edge. There is a fairly good track across most of it but it can be windy up there. Just watch the weather forecast and take suitable clothing. You can either loop round back to Glenridding or descend to Thirlmere at High Park Wood.

⑭ ★ **Great Gable.** Great Gable is another of the classic mountain climbs in the Lake District, and at 899 metres (2949 feet), it's not far behind the highest ones. Heading north from Wasdale Head, Great Gable rises up dramatically in front of you and you can ascend it via Sty Head. Alternatively, start from Seathwaite and go up along Sty Head Gill or Sour Milk Gill. There's a longer route in from Ennerdale Water (see above) continuing along the forest path after the lake, then up to the Windy Gap.

⑮ ★ **Blencathra.** Located northeast of Keswick, this mountain is also known as Saddleback, which is how

it appears from the east side. The usual starting point is from Threlkeld car park, with an ascent via Doddick Gill and towards the top, Sharp Edge, an exposed ridge. It's an achievement to get up this ridge with a scramble to the top, but from here you'll have views of the Solway Firth and even Scotland on a clear day.

⑯ ★ **The Old Man of Coniston.** This mountain looms dramatically over Coniston, but isn't as high as some of the other fells. Most walkers ascend along the path near Church Beck; from the top there are fantastic views of Coniston Water and south to Morecambe Bay.

⑰ ★ **High Street.** The ancient trade route of the Romans, High Street is a long walk along a flat plateau. There are several routes up to High Street, including from Askham, rising up Askham Fell. You can follow High Street south-west, eventually coming down into Troutbeck. A more popular route starts at Mardale Head (the road that runs along the length of Haweswater).

Multi-day Walks

⑱ ★ **Coast to Coast.** The most famous of Wainwright's walks (p 153), the Coast to Coast extends from St

Alfred Wainwright

If any name is associated with walking in the Lake District, it is that of Alfred Wainwright, whose *Pictorial Guides to the Fells* are the most celebrated walking guides for the region. Born in Blackburn, Lancashire in 1907, Wainwright became interested in walking from an early age. He fell in love with the Lake District when he first visited the area at the age of 23, and eventually moved there in 1941 when he took a job in Kendal. The unique feature of Wainwright's guides is his detailed handwritten accounts of the routes, accompanied by his idiosyncratic pen-and-ink maps and drawings of all that he could see on the way. As well as his *Pictorial Guides*, he wrote the *Pennine Way Companion* in 1968 followed by the *Coast to Coast Walk*, which he devised himself. His walking guides have been reissued and are available from most good booksellers and throughout the Lake District. He died from a heart attack in 1991 and his ashes were scattered at the top of Haystacks, a fell near Buttermere.

Bees on the Cumbrian coast to Robin Hood's Bay in North Yorkshire. You'll need around two weeks to walk the route, which passes through Ennerdale, Grasmere, Glenridding, Shap and Kirkby Stephen. There's also a cycling version that goes through Penrith and Alston. *St Bees to Robin Hood's Bay, 191 miles. 2 weeks.*

🕙 ★ **Cumbria Coastal Way.** As the name suggests, this route follows Cumbria's coastline. It starts (or ends) in Milnthorpe on the border with Lancashire and ends in Abbey Town in north-west Cumbria. You can hop on the train to avoid long treks round the estuaries, but the path takes you through Grange-over-Sands, Barrow-in-Furness, Ravenglass, Whitehaven, Maryport and Silloth. *Cumbrian coast, 124 miles, 8–10 days.*

🕘 ★ **The Cumbria Way.** You can walk this route in around a week, depending on your speed and fitness. Starting in Ulverston, in the South Lakes, it goes north through Coniston, Great Langdale, Keswick, Bassenthwaite and Caldbeck, ending

at Carlisle. *Ulverston to Carlisle. 70 miles. 1 week.*

The Sherpa Van Project can help you plan multi-day walks and will transport your luggage to your next accommodation. *29 The Green, Richmond, North Yorkshire.* ☎ *0871 5200124 (baggage);* ☎ *01609 883731 (accommodation). www. sherpavan.com.*

The view from the peak of Scafell Pike.

Best **Cycling**

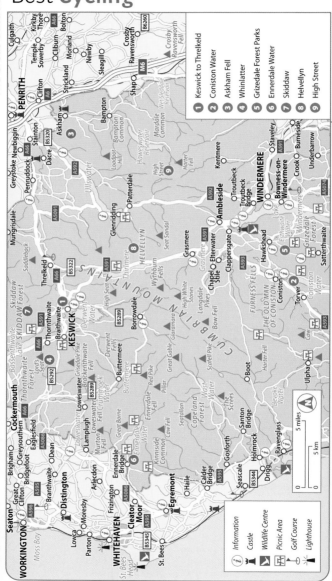

1. Keswick to Threlkeld
2. Coniston Water
3. Askham Fell
4. Whinlatter
5. Grizedale Forest Parks
6. Ennerdale Water
7. Skiddaw
8. Helvellyn
9. High Street

Information
Castle
Wildlife Centre
Picnic Area
Golf Course
Lighthouse

0   5 miles
0   5 km

Road cyclists and mountain bikers have been coming to the Lake District for years, making the most of the winding roads through spectacular scenery. And the opportunities for cycling are improving, thanks in part to the National Cycle Network's campaign for improved road and traffic-free routes. New off-road trails have opened in Grizedale and Whinlatter Forest Parks. The information below provides a few ideas for each category as well as information on bike hire and repair. Make sure you go well prepared with helmets, waterproofs, spare inner tubes, puncture repair kits, drinks and mobile phones.

Family Cycling

There are plenty of gentle routes suitable for children and those who want something more leisurely. For off-road cycling, follow the former railway path from ① **Keswick to Threlkeld** (3 miles) and back, explore the trails around ② **Coniston Water** or onto ③ **Askham Fell**. There are also some quiet way-marked trails through ④ **Whinlatter** and ⑤ **Grizedale Forest**

Parks (apart from the mountain biking ones below, which are more technical) as well as the forest path alongside ⑥ **Ennerdale Water**. The tourist office has a map of suggested cycle routes throughout the Lake District. You can also get information from the Lake District National Park, www.lake-district.gov.uk, and Sustrans—the National Cycle Network, www.sustrans.org.

There are family cycle paths throughout the Lake District.

The Great Outdoors

Lake District National Park

The **Lake District National Park** was established in 1951 to protect the landscape from unnecessary damage through a programme of conservation legislation and planning. It works in conjunction with The National Trust on some conservation projects, but the latter is a charity that owns several stately homes and parks, some of which fall within the national park boundaries. Most of the other land in the national park is privately owned. For more information on outdoor activities, visit the **Lake District Visitor Centre** at Brockhole, a large country mansion beside Lake Windermere. www.lake-district.gov.uk.

Mountain Biking

What mountain biker wouldn't be attracted to the extreme terrain of the Lake District's fells and forests? The Lake District is a protected national park with a delicate ecosystem. Still, there's an amazing network of trails taking in some spectacular scenery and providing as much challenge as you want. Mountain bikers can legally ride along **bridleways**, but **not footpaths.** Also, be aware that some bridleways aren't suitable due to the gradient, rocks and mud. There

Follow the National Cycle Network paths around the Lake District.

Mountain bikers can ride on bridleways.

are routes to **7** **Skiddaw**, **8** **Helvellyn** and **9** **High Street** if you're looking for a challenge. The best thing to do is buy an OS (Ordnance Survey) map and seek advice at local bike shops regarding routes, safety and equipment.

Two areas with dedicated mountain-biking devised routes are **Whinlatter Forest Park** and **Grizedale Forest Park**, www.forestry.gov.uk/whinlatterhome and www.forestry.gov.uk/grizedalehome, which combine single track biking with twists, descents and jumps. You have to look out for other mountain bikers but horses and walkers have their own trails.

Serious road cyclists tackle steep passes like Kirkstone.

Road Cycling & Touring

The Lake District is very popular with road cyclists/tourers as there are hundreds of miles of quiet roads to explore. The A6, A590, A5092, A595 and A66 travel all the way round the edge of the Lake District (134 miles in total) from Penrith south to Kendal, west to Silecroft, north all the way along the coast and east back to Penrith via Cockermouth and Keswick. For shorter road routes, there are circular lakeside roads taking in Windermere and Coniston Water (35 miles), Ullswater and Thirlmere (46 miles), Derwentwater, Buttermere and Crummock Water (27 miles), as well as quieter forest roads through Whinlatter and Grizedale Forest Parks and mountain passes such as Kirkstone, Hardknott and Wrynose. There's also the Coast-to-Coast cycle route, which starts in Whitehaven and ends in Tynemouth, travelling through Penrith and Alston. Study a map and plan your route according to your ability and strengths.

Bike Hire & Repair

Ambleside
Bike Treks, *Rydal Road, Ambleside.* ☎ *015394 31245. www.bike treks.net.*
Grizedale Forest Park
Grizedale Mountain Bikes, *Grizedale Visitor Centre.* ☎ *01229 860369. www.grizedalemountainbikes.co.uk.*
Keswick
Lakeland Pedlar, *Bell Close, Keswick.* ☎ *017687 74492. www. lakelandpedlar.co.uk.*
Penrith
Eden Cycle Hire Brougham Hill, *Penrith.* ☎ *01768 840400. www. edencyclecentre.co.uk.*
Windermere and Newby Bridge
Country Lanes, *The Railway Station, Windermere.* ☎ *015394 44544 and Lakeside* ☎ *07748 512286. www.countrylaneslake district.co.uk.*

Best Outdoor **Sport & Adventure**

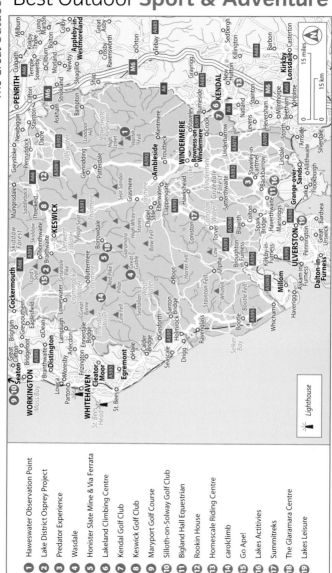

1. Haweswater Observation Point
2. Lake District Osprey Project
3. Predator Experience
4. Wasdale
5. Honister Slate Mine & Via Ferrata
6. Lakeland Climbing Centre
7. Kendal Golf Club
8. Keswick Golf Club
9. Maryport Golf Course
10. Silloth-on-Solway Golf Club
11. Bigland Hall Equestrian
12. Rookin House
13. Homescale Riding Centre
14. carolclimb
15. Go Ape!
16. Lakes Actitivies
17. Summitreks
18. The Glaramara Centre
19. Lakes Leisure

* Lighthouse

I t makes sense that most of the Lake District's activities take place outdoors. Expert ornithologists, climbers and even golfers come to pursue their pastime. But it's also the perfect place to try something new, and there's a whole host of companies geared up to show you how. Kids might like the high-wire adventures at Go Ape in Whinlatter and Grizedale Forest Parks and adults can enjoy the thrill of the *via ferrata* climbing cables in Honister Slate Mine. Horse lovers can enjoy days trotting through woodland, but if you're after something more sedate, opt for birdwatching, fishing and a round of golf.

Birdwatching

With over 200 species of bird in the Lake District, experienced birdwatchers will be in their element and can head off on their own. On the fells, you can see migrant species such as Ring Ouzel, which arrive in spring, or Ravens, Buzzards and Peregrines throughout the year. Around Haweswater, you might spot England's only pair of nesting Golden Eagles. Of course, the Lake District also has usual woodland birds such as flycatchers, woodpeckers and Sparrowhawks, and lakeside favourites like waterfowl, ducks and Dippers, but one of the main attractions are the Ospreys (see below).

The forest parks are full of small birds.

❶ Haweswater Observation Point. Your best chance of seeing the Golden Eagles is from the RSPB observation point open between April and August. It is located 1.5 miles along a track from the car park at the southern end of the only road that leads along Haweswater. *RSPB.* ☎ *01931 713376. www.rspb.org.uk.*

❷ Lake District Osprey Project. Founded to ensure the successful breeding of Ospreys at Bassenthwaite Lake, the Lake District Osprey Project gives the public an opportunity to see and learn about the birds. There's an informational exhibition on the project at the visitor centre in Whinlatter Forest Park. You can see the Ospreys for yourself at Dodd Wood, by Bassenthwaite Lake, where there are two viewing points. With the help of high-powered telescopes, you might catch them fishing in the lake and feeding, flying and washing. The Osprey Bus runs from Keswick to both the exhibition and the Dodd Wood viewing points. ☎ *017687 78469. www.osprey watch.co.uk.*

❸ Predator Experience. Here's the chance to spot different birds of prey and even take some falconry tuition. There are various experience days including watching Golden Eagles on the fells and guided walks around Windermere to spot hawks. *Greenacre, Newby Bridge.* ☎ *07500 956348. www. predatorexperience.co.uk.*

The Great Outdoors

Hiking the summit ridge of Blencathra.

Climbing & Scrambling

There are hundreds of rock faces with public access, suitable for climbers with some or plenty of experience. Ambleside is a favourite base for climbers, with several climbs in the Langdale Pikes, but if you're not after nightlife then
4 Wasdale is the place to go, where you'll have the full mountain experience. There are other climbs close to Buttermere, Coniston, Glenridding and Keswick, with a mix of roadside and easy-to-reach climbs. For more information on climbs in each destination, see the Tourist

You'll find osprey information at Whinlatter Visitor Centre.

Office website, www.lakedistrict
outdoors.co.uk.

There are also plenty of courses for beginners, indoor climbing walls to practise on and the via ferrata experience (see below), which is a good way for younger and less-experienced climbers to start.

5 Honister Slate Mine & Via Ferrata. The via ferrata is a system of cables and footholds that allows the novice to traverse and climb sheer rock faces. Honister Slate Mine's version of the system, first set up in the Dolomites in the First World War, has been so successful since it opened in 2008 that it now has two routes. The second one has a zip wire that whizzes you straight from one rock face to another. You're kitted out with a harness and helmet and taken out by a qualified climbing instructor. The most difficult parts for me were the 'ladder', several footholds that go up vertically and are a strain on the arms; and the 'bridge', a horizontal ladder-like crossing with nothing to hold onto. You're relying on your legs, but remember you are still clipped on! Make sure you book ahead during peak season to avoid disappointment, especially if there's a group of you. *Honister Pass, Borrowdale.*

☎ 021 3912800. www.honister-slate-mine.co.uk. Admission mine tours £9.75 adults; £4.75 under 16 yrs; via ferrata classic £25 adults; £20 children; via ferrata zip wire £35 adults; £25 under 16 yrs; all-day pass classic £37 adults; £28 under 16 yrs; £125 family (2 + 2); all-day zip wire £48 adults; £34 under 16 yrs; £160 family. Open daily 9am–5pm. Stagecoach Rambler 78.

⑥ Lakeland Climbing Centre.
The largest centre in the Lake District, there are courses for beginners as well as for more experienced climbers and boulderers. After you've practised and got a little confidence on the indoor walls, the centre can organize some outdoor trips, including taster days and private guiding. *Lake District Business Park, Kendal.* ☎ *01539 721766.* *www.kendalwall.co.uk.*

Golf
There are several golf courses in Cumbria but I have listed the ones below for a a range of locations, woodland, riverside, fellside and links (coastal) courses.

⑦ Kendal Golf Club. This veteran par-70 course has an elevated position overlooking the town and

Children can learn to climb indoors.

the Westmorland Fells, with challenges for all levels of golfer. *The Heights, Kendal.* ☎ *01539 733708.* *www.kendalgolfclub.co.uk.*

⑧ Keswick Golf Club. Located east of Derwentwater, on Threlkeld Common, this course has a glorious mountain backdrop with Blencathra rising up to the north. The 18-hole, par-71 course is designed to test all levels with various hazards and tree-lined fairways. *Threlkeld Hall, Threlkeld, Keswick.* ☎ *017687 79324. www.keswickgolfclub.com.*

⑨ Maryport Golf Course. This well-established 18-hole course

Not for the faint-hearted – climbing Napes Needle, at Great Gable.

Honister Slate Mine offers tours and a taste of climbing.

faces the Solway Firth with views of Scotland on a clear day; a part links, part parkland course. *Bankend, Maryport.* ☎ *01900 812605. www. maryportgolfclub.co.uk.*

⑩ Silloth-on-Solway Golf Club.
This stunning coastal course has views of the hills of Galloway in Scotland, the Isle of Man and the Lake District fells. A championship links course, it has 18 holes with bunkers, sandy dunes, wooded fairways and firm greens. *Station Road, Silloth, Wigton.* ☎ *016973 31304. www.sillothgolfclub.co.uk.*

Horseriding & Pony Trekking
⑪ Bigland Hall Equestrian.
Offers riding holidays and individual

classes. Located at Backbarrow, south of Windermere, the centre gives you the chance to ride through some challenging terrain. Younger riders and families can stick to riding on the estate, while experienced riders can gallop across Morecambe Bay sands or enjoy days out in the fells. *Backbarrow, near Newby Bridge* ☎ *015395 30333. www.biglandhall.com.*

⑫ Rookin House.
Here is an equestrian and activity centre with a wide range of activities from pony trekking to archery, children's assault courses to a zip wire and go karts. *Rookin House Farm, Troutbeck, Ullswater. Penrith* ☎ *017684 83561. www.rookinhouse.co.uk.*

⑬ Homescale Riding Centre.
This family-run BHS (British Horse Society)-approved riding centre near Kendal runs courses for anyone over 5 years old and will pair you with a suitable horse. As well as the classes, you can enjoy private trekking and hacking sessions. *Peter and Eleanor Jones, Old Hutton, near Kendal.* ☎ *01539 729388. www. holmescalesridingcentre.co.uk.*

Outdoor Adventure
⑭ carolclimb.
An all-round adventure experience. You can go mountaineering, climbing and walking as

Maryport and Silloth golf courses look onto the Solway Firth.

There's pony trekking and horseriding for all levels.

well as kayaking and angling. You can also take certificates in navigation and as a Mountain Leader. *Low Gillerthwaite Field Centre, Ennerdale, Cleator.* ☎ *01946 862342. www. carolclimb.co.uk.*

⑮ Go Ape! A high-wire adventure that allows you to swing through the trees on zip wires, walk across rope bridges and take a Tarzan swing. There are two centres in Cumbria, one in Grizedale and the other in Whinlatter Forest Park. ☎ *0845 6439215. www.goape.co.uk.*

⑯ Lakes Activities. A range of activities around the Lake District, including archery, off-road driving in 4x4 and all-terrain vehicles, horseriding, go-karting, clay pigeon shooting, raft building, team challenge days and much more. ☎ *015395 35999. www.lakesactivities.co.uk.*

⑰ Summitreks. This is a multi-adventure company that offers a combination of rock climbing, scrambling and children's adventure days with watersports and raft building. *Unit 2, Lake Road, Coniston.* ☎ *015394 41212. www.summitreks. co.uk.*

⑱ The Glaramara Centre. At the head of the Borrowdale valley is this residential outdoor activities centre. There's everything from abseiling to orienteering and Viking boating. *Seatoller, Borrowdale.* ☎ *017687 77222. www.glaramara. co.uk.*

Tennis
⑲ Lakes Leisure. Lakes Leisure has a large tennis centre at its Ulverston branch with qualified coaches. It also has eight courts for mini-tennis, and for all courts you can pay and play, including the hire of equipment, if you don't have your own. *Priory Road, Ulverston,* ☎ *01229 584110. www.lakesleisure.org.uk.*

Fly through the trees at Go Ape!

Best **Watersports**

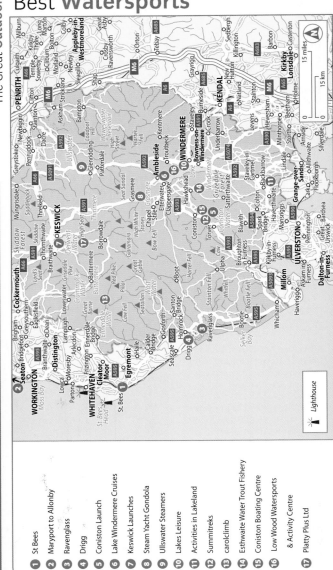

* Lighthouse

1 St Bees
2 Maryport to Allonby
3 Ravenglass
4 Drigg
5 Coniston Launch
6 Lake Windermere Cruises
7 Keswick Launches
8 Steam Yacht Gondola
9 Ullswater Steamers
10 Lakes Leisure
11 Activities in Lakeland
12 Summitreks
13 carolclimb
14 Esthwaite Water Trout Fishery
15 Coniston Boating Centre
16 Low Wood Watersports
& Activity Centre
17 Platty Plus Ltd

With 16 Lakes and over 150 miles of coastline, there's plenty of opportunity for watersports. The easiest way to enjoy the water is on the ferry and steam boats that cross Coniston Water, Derwentwater, Windermere and Ullswater. There are also places to take your own canoe, kayak and yacht, places to hire equipment and take a course, and several beaches along the coast.

Best Beaches

You won't find built-up seaside resorts along the Cumbrian coastline but quiet coastal towns, and several stretches of deserted sands. My favourite beach on the Cumbrian coast is ❶ **St Bees**; when the tide goes out you're spoiled with smooth sand perfect for building castles. North of ❷ **Maryport to Allonby**, there are long sandy stretches facing the Solway Firth. Pretty ❸ **Ravenglass** lies at the convergence of three rivers, which then lead into the sea. The sand dunes between here and ❹ **Drigg** are part of a nature reserve, rich in flora and fauna.

Boat Trips

There are independent companies operating on several lakes; the boats are possibly the best way to take in the beauty of the lakes without too much effort.

❺ **Coniston Launch.** *See p 141.*

❻ **Lake Windermere Cruises.** *See p 12,* ❶.

❼ **Keswick Launches.** *See p 136,* ❽.

❽ **Steam Yacht Gondola.** *See p 116,* ❹.

❾ **Ullswater Steamers.** *See p 177.*

Canoeing, Kayaking & Windsurfing

There are several centres where you can hire equipment or take a class. ❿ **Lakes Leisure** offers canoeing, kayaking and windsurfing classes and multi-activity days. You can even gain certificates, and there are special activities for kids. *Leigh Groves Building, Rayrigg Road, Windermere. ☎ 015394 47183. www. lakesleisure.org.uk).*

⓫ **Activities in Lakeland.** Organize two-hour sessions in Canadian canoes and Eskimo kayaks canoeing on Windermere or Coniston Water. ☎ *015395 35999. www. lakesactivities.co.uk.*

If you want to combine some kayaking with land-based activities like climbing, then opt for companies like ⓬ **Summitreks** or ⓭ **carolclimb** (see p 162).

Hop on and off Keswick launches to explore Derwentwater.

There are sailing courses on several lakes.

Fishing

You can choose from freshwater fishing and sea fishing in the Lake District and there are plenty of angling clubs and fisheries throughout the region, as well as tackle shops. Choose from game fishing in lakes for brown and rainbow trout, charr, perch and pike; game fishing in rivers for salmon and sea trout; and course fishing for pike, carp,

The boats are ready to take out at Bowness.

tench and bream. Inland you'll either have to go to a fishery or buy a rod licence, which are available from the post office or online for one or eight days, or for a full season—see www.environment-agency.gov.uk/subjects/fish. Several hotels have corporate licences, so you can just stay there and fish. These include Rothay Manor Hotel The Salutation in Ambleside (p 101 and p 99), The Low Wood Hotel and Watersports Centre on the banks of Lake Windermere (p 167), the Kings Arms Hotel (p 132) in Hawkshead and Gilpin Lodge Hotel (p 105), near Windermere. For more information on fishing in the Lake District, see www.lakedistrictfishing.net.

⑭ Esthwaite Water Trout Fishery. Wind down for a while at this quiet lake west of Windermere. It's the largest stocked lake in north-west England. You can hire a boat and tackle or buy what you need from the shop. Novices can take fishing tuition, or maybe you're a dab hand and would like to take part in a competition—see their website for details. *Cockermouth.* ☎ *015394 36541. www.hawksheadtrout.com. Open daily 9am–6pm (5pm in winter).*

Sailing

From Windermere to Ullswater, Coniston to Derwentwater, you can go sailing on several of the lakes, take a course or hire a dinghy or larger yacht.

⑮ Coniston Boating Centre. Next to the launches, you can hire rowing boats, electric self-drive boats, canoes, kayaks and dinghies. They also run RYA level 1 and 2 sailing courses. *Lake Road, Coniston.* ☎ *015394 41366. www.lake-district. gov.uk.*

Lakes Leisure. You can take introductory courses on Windermere with Lakes Leisure (see above for details) as well as more advanced seamanship and racing training. They also hire out dinghies for those with RYA Level 2 qualifications.

⑯ Low Wood Watersports & Activity Centre. This large watersports centre is attached to the Low

Take someone strong to help with the rowing.

Wood Hotel on Windermere. They run sailing and other watersports courses accredited by the Royal Yachting Association, British Canoe Union and British Water Ski. If you don't want or need a course, you can hire motorboats, canoes and kayaks, rowing boats, dinghies and even a Hunter 19 keelboat. *Low*

Windermere lake has several marinas and watersports centres.

You can enjoy gentle days on the water in Ullswater.

Wood ☎ *015394 39441. www.elh. co.uk/watersports.*

⑰ Platty Plus Ltd. Based on Derwentwater, Platty Plus offer dinghy sailing courses, as well as seamanship, spinnaker sailing and young sailors' schemes. There's also powerboating, kayaking and canoeing instruction on offer. *Lodore Boat Landings, Derwentwater* ☎ *017687 76572. www.plattyplus.co.uk.*

Swimming
Lakes Leisure has a 25-metre heated indoor swimming pool

at Kendal, as well as a smaller learner pool. Ulverston also has a 25-metre pool. *Burton Road, Kendal* ☎ *015397 29777 or Priory Road, Ulverston,* ☎ *01229 584110. www. lakesleisure.org.uk.*

Sports & Leisure Centres
Lakes Leisure has a watersports centre on Windermere, tennis, swimming and other activities at Ulverston, and swimming, aerobics, spectator sports and theatre at Kendal. See above. ●

The
Savvy Traveller

Before You Go

Cumbria's Tourist Information Centres & Visitor Centres

Ambleside Central Buildings, Market Cross, Ambleside ☎ 015394 32582 email: info@thehubofambleside.com; www.amblesideonline.co.uk.

Appleby Moot Hall, Borough-gate, Appleby-in-Westmorland, Cumbria, CA16 6XD ☎ 017683 51177 email: tic@applebytown.org.uk; www.applebytown.talktalk business.net.

Barrow W 28, Duke Street, Barrow-in-Furness, Cumbria, LA14 1HU ☎ 01229 876505 email:tourist info@barrowbc.gov.uk; www.barrowtourism.co.uk

Bowness Bay, Glebe Road, Bowness-on-Windermere, Windermere, Cumbria, LA23 3HJ ☎ 015394 42895 email:bownesstic @lake-district.gov.uk.

Brockhole Lake District Visitor, Centre Windermere LA23 1LJ ☎ 015394 46601 email: infodesk@lake-district.gov.uk; www.lake-district.gov.uk.

Carlisle Old Town Hall, Green Market, Carlisle, Cumbria, CA3 8JD ☎ 01228 625600 email: tourism@carlisle-city.gov.uk; www.historic-carlisle.org.

Cockermouth Town Hall, Market Street, Cockermouth, CA13 9NP ☎ 01900 822634 email: cockermouthtic@co-net.com; www.cockermouth.org.uk.

Coniston Ruskin Avenue, Coniston, LA21 8EH ☎ 015394 41533 email: mail@conistontic.org; www.conistontic.org.

Egremont Lowes Court Gallery and Egremont Tourist Information Centre, 12 Main Street, Egremont CA22 2DW ☎ 01946 820693 email: lowescourt@bt connect.com; www.visitegremont.co.uk.

Grange-over-Sands Victoria Hall, Main Street, Grange-over-Sands, LA11 6DP ☎ 015395 34026 email: grangetic@southlakeland.gov.uk; www.grangeoversands.net.

Hawkshead Main Street, Hawkshead, Cumbria, LA22 0NT ☎ 015394 36946 email: enquiries@hawksheadtouristinfo.org.uk; www.hawksheadtouristinfo.org.uk.

Kendal Town Hall, Highgate, Kendal, LA9 4DL ☎ 01539 725758 email: kendaltic@southlakeland.gov.uk; www.kendaltowncouncil.gov.uk.

Keswick Market Square, Keswick, Cumbria, CA12 5JR ☎ 07687 72645 email: tourism@keswick.org; www.keswick.org.

Maryport Irish Street, Maryport, Cumbria, CA15 8AD ☎ 01900 811450 email: info@thewave maryport.co.uk; www.thewave maryport.co.uk.

Millom Council Centre, St.Georges Road, Millom, LA18 4DD ☎ 01946 598914 email: millomtic@copelandbc.gov.uk; www.millom.org.uk.

Penrith Robinson's School, Middlegate, Penrith, Cumbria, CA11 7PT ☎ 01768 867466 email: pen.tic@eden.gov.uk; www.visiteden.co.uk.

Southwaite M6 Service Area, Southwaite, Carlisle, Cumbria, CA4 0NS ☎ 016974 73445.

Ullswater Main Car Park, Glenridding, CA11 0PA ☎ 017684 82414 email: ullswatertic@lake-district.gov.uk; www.ullswater.co.uk.

Ulverston Coronation Hall, County Square, Ulverston, LA12 7LZ ☎ 01229 587120 email: ulverstontic@southlakeland.gov.uk; www.ulverston.net.

Useful Websites

The official tourism website for Cumbria Tourism is www.go
lakes.co.uk and for the **Lake District National Park** www.lake-
district.gov.uk, which provides information on rambling, scrambling, guided walks, watersports and events. You'll also find extra
attraction information on www.visitcumbria.com. District council
websites can also be helpful for localized accommodation and
events, including www.southlakeland.gov.uk (from Coniston down
to Ulverston) and www.eden.gov.uk/tourism (from Ullswater east-
wards). There is also a website dedicated to the western Lake District, www.western-lakedistrict.co.uk. See www.nationaltrust.org.
uk for information on National Trust stately homes, parks and other
property in the Lake District, and www.english-heritage.org.uk
for English Heritage properties. As well as the tourist office websites, there are several covering accommodation, including www.
discoverthelakes.co.uk, www.staylakedistrict.co.uk and www.lake-
district.com.

Whitehaven Market Hall,
Market Place, Whitehaven, Cumbria,
CA28 7JG ☎ 01946 598914 email:
tic@copelandbc.gov.uk; www.
whitehaven.org.uk

Windermere Victoria Street,
Windermere, LA23 1AD ☎ 015394
46499 email: windermeretic@
southlakeland.gov.uk; www.visit
windermere.co.uk.

Workington, 21 Finkle Street,
Workington, CA14 2BE ☎ 01900
606699 email: workingtontic@
allerdale.gov.uk; www.western-lake
district.co.uk.

Visa Information
Entry visas are not required for
stays of less than three months by
anyone holding a passport from
other European Union countries,
Switzerland, some Commonwealth
countries including Australia, Canada and New Zealand and some
non- European countries including
Japan and the USA. For full information on visas and entry into the UK,
check the website of the UK Border
Agency, www.ukvisas.gov.uk, well
in advance of your visit.

The Best Times to Go
The Lake District is a popular destination throughout the year for walkers, families and stag and hen
weekends; many go for short
breaks, but some stay for longer
holidays. Book ahead if you're coming from March to October. There
are generally more tourists during
this period, but if there's a sudden
heat wave, visitors come to the Lake
District on impulse. Also, check to
see what festivals are taking place
as the town of your choice might be
booked up months ahead.

During the summer holidays
you'll need to book campsites and
caravan parks too. For quiet get-
aways, come outside of the holidays
or during the winter months, when
you can hole up in a cottage or
hotel for less than in the summer.
Take note though, cottage rentals
are popular over the New Year.

Public Holidays

England has eight public holidays. On these days, banks, most offices and a few shops are closed.

New Year's Day—1st January
Good Friday—March/April
Easter Monday—March/April
Early May Bank Holiday—1st Monday in May
Spring Bank Holiday—last Monday in May
Summer Bank Holiday—last Monday in August
Christmas Day—25th December
Boxing Day—26th December

Festivals & Events

FEB. **Keswick Film Festival** Started by the local film club, this festival screens films from around the world at various Keswick venues. www.keswickfilmfestival.org.

MAR. **Cumbria Open Studios** First run over Easter weekend in 2009, this event gives visitors the chance to see artists at work in their studios throughout the county. It promotes the artists and inspires others, so the organizers hope it will return each spring.

MAY. **Keswick Jazz Festival** For four days in May, the town is buzzing with big bands and jazz soloists. Musicians from the UK and abroad play at various venues around town. www.keswickjazzfestival.co.uk.

Keswick Mountain Festival Come during this May festival to join experienced leaders and other outdoor enthusiasts on some classic fell walks, scrambles, climbs, nature trails and mountain bike rides. You can learn a few essential map-reading skills or grab the chance to hear a few tales from renowned adventurers. There are a few competitive events too, including orienteering and a triathlon. www.keswick mountainfestival.co.uk.

Festival of Fishing Anglers will be in their element at this fishing festival with fly rodding, river and boat fishing and plenty of tips from the pros. Suitable for beginners and more experienced anglers. www. gofishinglakedistrict.co.uk.

Festival of Fools During the week of the Spring Bank Holiday, Muncaster Castle becomes the site of madness as people compete to become the Fool of Muncaster. There are jesters, comedians and fools aplenty. www.muncaster. co.uk.

JUN. **Appleby Horse Fair** For a week every June, the village of Appleby-in-Westmorland fills with horses and is one of the largest gatherings of Gypsies and Travellers in the UK. Sunday is the main day with horse races and a fair. www. applebyfair.org

Whitehaven Maritime Festival This biennial event celebrates Whitehaven's maritime heritage with gusto. Expect tall ships, yachts and jet ski displays, as well as live music, a festival atmosphere around the harbor and special visitors like the Red Arrows. www.thefestival. org.uk

Woolfest A typically rural festival, you can learn everything there is to know about sheep's wool here. You can buy readymade sweaters, naturally dyed yarns and even fleeces to take home. www.woolfest.co.uk.

JUL. **Brampton Live** Just a half-hour drive from the Lakes, in northern Cumbria, this festival features a range of live folk music and dance. There's a craft tent for kids and food and clothing stalls, and the whole family can join in with the dancing at the ceilidh. www.bramptonlive.net.

Grasmere Rushbearing Festival This annual July event relives an

AVERAGE TEMPERATURE & RAINFALL

	JAN	FEB	MAR	APR	MAY	JUNE
Monthly Rain (MM)	93	78	63	73	58	56
Maximum Temp. (°C)	8.5	9	11	14	17	18
Minimum temp. (°C)	-3.5	-3.5	-2.5	-1.5	1.5	4.5

	JULY	AUG	SEPT	OCT	NOV	DEC
Monthly Rain (MM)	47	68	73	132	124	108
Maximum Temp. (°C)	20	20	17	14.5	14.5	9.5
Minimum temp. (°C)	6.5	6.5	4.5	2	-1	-2.5

age-old English tradition of strewing reeds on the old earthen floors of local churches. A procession of musicians and children carrying a cross of reeds leads through the village to the church.

Windermere Airshow July's peace is pierced as the planes fly over Bowness, but what a sight! This family event pulls in the crowds who come to see aerobatic displays, RAF parachute jumps and everything from spitfires and hawks to Chinook helicopters. www.windermere-rotary.org.uk.

Lake District Summer Music For two weeks from the end of July, there are concerts and events throughout the county. Expect Indian raga, organ recitals, piano masterclasses and opera from Ullswater to Ulverston. www.ldsm.org.uk.

AUG. **Solfest** This music festival takes place over the August Bank Holiday, north of Maryport, at Tarns. It attracts renowned indie, punk, rock and folk bands. Book ahead www.solwayfestival.co.uk.

SEPT. **Helvellyn Triathlon** This event is extreme! Yes, you need to be in peak condition, as it starts with a one-mile swim in cold Ullswater, followed by a 38-mile cycle (that includes the Kirkstone Pass) and ends with a nine-mile run up Helvellyn. Phew! www.trihard.co.uk/HelvellynHome.htm.

Sedburgh Festival of Books & Drama A few miles east of Kendal, Sedburgh is England's 'book town', with plenty of book shops and businesses. This festival celebrates with the latest book releases, drama and talks by famous authors. www.sedburgh.org.uk.

OCT. **Halloween & Darkest Muncaster** During Halloween week, you can go on spooky ghost tours of Muncaster Castle, if you dare. There are also daily magic shows and fire jugglers. Lights, music, sound and special effects illuminate the castle walls after dark when you can warm up with hot chocolate from the café! www.muncaster.co.uk.

NOV. **Coniston Power Boat Records Week** Everything from tiny hydroplanes to the largest offshore boats come to Coniston Water, the site of many a water-speed record attempt. The drivers hope to end the racing season by getting into the record books themselves. www.conistonpowerboatrecords.co.uk.

DEC. **Keswick Traditional Christmas Fayre** This is the perfect place to pick up a few stocking fillers, while enjoying the Christmas lights and entertainment. Every stall here aims to raise money for good causes.

The Weather

The Lake District has a changeable climate but is one of the wettest regions in England. The coastal areas are usually milder in the winter, while the mountain temperature tends to be at the minimum end of the scale. In summer you might have scorching days in the valleys but don't under-estimate how much colder it will be higher up. In addition, the weather can change in minutes with high winds, hill fog and even snow descending rapidly. Lakeland roads can be subject to flooding, so make sure you check the weather conditions before you make plans. For an up-to-date weather forecast ☎ 0870 055 0575 or see www.metoffice.gov.uk.

Cellphones

Signal strength for cellphones (called mobile phones in the UK) tends to vary in the Lake District, due to the remoteness of some areas. There are blackspots in the fells, so don't rely on mobile phones in an emergency (take GPS equipment if you're undertaking any hazardous activities in a remote area, especially if you are alone). In lower lying, well-populated areas, reception is usually fine.

UK sim cards can be bought at mobile phone shops and at some supermarkets, which allow you to receive calls free of charge. They cost £6–£10 and can be topped up with prepaid vouchers.

For more information on phones and fell walking, see our Strategies chapter (p 10).

Getting **There**

By Plane

Blackpool Airport (☎ 0871 8556868 www.blackpool international.com) is 61 miles south of Windermere). For flight enquires ☎ 0871 8556868. This small airport schedules several domestic and European flights. Take the sprinter train to Preston for connecting services to the Lake District.

Glasgow Airport (☎ 0870 0400008 www.glasgowairport.com) is located 149 miles north of Windermere). For flight enquires ☎ 0870 0400008. Both domestic and international airlines operate from this airport. Take a train and change at Glasgow Central Station for the Lake District (see below).

Liverpool John Lennon Airport (☎ 0871 5218484 www.liverpoolairport.com) is located 94 miles south of Windermere). For flight enquires ☎ 0906 1088484. Both domestic and international

airlines operate in and out of here. Travel by bus to Liverpool for connecting services to the Lake District.

Manchester Airport (☎ 08712 710711 www.manchesterairport.co.uk) is located 88 miles south of Windermere). For flight enquires ☎ 09010 101000. This is the third-largest airport in the UK, serving both domestic and international airlines. There are direct train and bus services to the Lake District.

Newcastle Airport (☎ 0871 8821122 www.newcastleairport.com) is 88 miles north-east of Windermere). For flight enquires ☎ 0871 8821131. Domestic and international airlines fly to and from here. Travel on the Metro light railway to Newcastle Central station, where there are connecting services to the Lake District.

The following airlines fly to one or more of the above airports. Check their websites for full details on schedules and services.

In addition to these there are several charter flights — see the airport websites for details.

Aer Aaran www.aeraaran.com
Aer Lingus www.aerlingus.ie
Air Berlin www.airberlin.com
Air France www.airfrance.com
Air Malta www.airmalta.com
Air Southwest www.airsouthwest.com
Air Transat www.airtransat.ca
Alitalia www.alitalia.com
American Airlines www.aa.com
Aurigny www.aurigny.com
Bmi www.flybmi.com
Bmi baby www.bmibaby.com
British Airways www.ba.com
Bulgaria Air www.air.bg
Canadian Affair www.canadianaffair.com
City Airline www.cityairline.com
Continental www.continental.com
CSA Czech www.csa.cz
Cyprus www.cyprusairways.com
Delta Airlines www.delta.com
Eastern Airways www.easternairways.com
EasyJet www.easyjet.com
Emirates www.emirates.com
Etihad www.etihadairways.com
Finnair www.finnair.com
Flybe www.flybe.com
Iceland Air www.icelandair.co.uk
KLM www.klm.com
Libyan Arab Airlines Libyanarabairline.com
Lufthansa www.lufthansa.com
Monarch www.flymonarch.com
Olympic Airlines www.olympicairlines.com
Pakistan Int Airlines www.piac.com.pk
Qatar www.qatarairways.com
Ryanair www.ryanair.com
SAS Scandinavian www.scandinavian.net
Saudi Arabian Airlines www.saudiairlines.com
Singapore Airlines www.singaporeair.com
Swiss International Airlines www.swiss.com
Turkish Airlines www.thy.com
US Airways www.usairways.com
Virgin Atlantic Airways www.virgin-atlantic.com
VLM www.flyvlm.com

By Train

Several train lines operate in the Lake District, including **Virgin Trains** (www.virgintrains.co.uk) from London and the south of England to Carlisle and Glasgow, stopping at Penrith and Oxenholme in the Lake District. **FirstTranspennine Express** (www.tpexpress.co.uk) runs services from Edinburgh Haymarket to Oxenholme, Penrith and Morecambe Bay. **Northern Rail** (www.northernrail.org), stops at Oxenholme, travelling partly via the scenic Carlisle Settle railway route, or up from Manchester to Grange-over-Sands and Ulverston (on the Furness Line), along the east coast through Ravenglass, Whitehaven and Maryport.

By Coach

The most frequent service is operated by **National Express** (www.nationalexpress.co.uk), with services from most of the main UK and Scottish cities. They also stop at some of the smaller places with no train station. Time from London to Kendal is approximately 6 hours. Consult **Traveline** (☎ 0870 2002233, www.traveline.org.uk) for more complicated or out-of-the-way routes.

By Sea

Ferry services operate from Dublin to Liverpool and Holyhead, Belfast to Stranraer (or Larne to Cairnryan), the Isle of Man to Heysham, and Holland to Newcastle.

DFDS Seaways www.dfdsseaways.co.uk
Irish Ferries www.irishferries.com
P&O Irish Sea Ferries www.poirishsea.com

Steam Packet Company www.steam-packet.com
Stena Line www.stenaline.co.uk

By Car

Many visitors travel to the Lake District by car, which can be useful if you're staying somewhere more remote. The M6 motorway runs all the way from Birmingham in the south to Carlisle in the north. Exit at J36 for the South Lakes and Kendal, J37 for Kendal, Windermere and Ambleside (via the A591), J39 for Shap and J40 for Penrith. The A66 runs west from here to Keswick and Cockermouth, and the A595 from Carlisle direct to Cockermouth. The A595 runs from Workington and Whitehaven south along the Cumbrian coastline to Dalton-in-Furness. From here, the A590 runs across the South Lakes back to the M6. The A6 is an alternative, scenic route from Penrith to Kendal.

Getting **Around**

Although a car can be convenient, it's not absolutely essential for getting around the Lake District. Several useful bus services operate here, and some very scenic train routes.

By Bus

There are several 'Rambler' routes taking scenic routes through the Lake District:

Borrowdale Rambler (78) from Keswick.

Coniston Rambler (505) from Windermere to Coniston via Ambleside.

Honister Rambler (77/77A) a circular route from Keswick through Whinlatter, Borrowdale and Honister Pass.

Kentmere Rambler (519), which passes through Staveley on the way to Ambleside.

Kirkstone Rambler from Bowness-on-Windermere to Glenridding (Ullswater).

Langdale Rambler (516) from Ambleside to Dungeon Ghyll.

In addition, there are other useful and scenic bus rides:

Cross Lakes Shuttle from Bowness to Coniston via Grizedale Forest and Hawkshead.

Lakeslink (555) from Lancaster to Carlisle via Kendal, Windermere and Keswick.

Open Top Lakeland Experience (The Lakes Rider) (599) from Bowness to Grasmere.

Osprey Bus from Keswick to Mirehouse and Dodd Wood.

Patterdale Bus (108) from Penrith to Patterdale.

Ullswater Connexion (208) from Keswick to Patterdale.

For other bus routes, see www.stagecoachbus.com or call Traveline on ☎ 0871 2002233. Stagecoach offers a Megarider ticket, which can save you money if you're going to be using the bus a great deal.

Explorer tickets can be used on the entire north-west network, cost £9.75 adults, £6.50 children, £5.90 seniors. Dayrider tickets are valid in specific areas: Kendal £1.80, Whitehaven £2.20.

The Mountain Goat is a private company that organizes holidays as well as daily/weekly tours around the Lake District. These include tours of the most spectacular lakes, high passes, Beatrix Potter countryside and South and East Lakes tours. Victoria Street, Windermere. ☎ 015394 45161. www.mountain-goat.com.

By Train
There are several historic and scenic railway lines in the Lake District, which use vintage steam engines.

Lakeside & Haverthwaite Railway
Steam railway between Lakeside at the southern end of Lake Windermere and Haverthwaite in the Leven Valley. ☎ 015395 31594. www.lakesiderailway.co.uk Admission £5.70/£3.45 adult return/single; £2.85/£2.30 child return/single; £15.50 family ticket. First and last trains Haverthwaite 10.40am/3.10pm (4.15pm peak season); Lakeside 11.15am/3.45pm (4.50pm peak season).

Ravenglass & Eskdale Railway
Seven-mile narrow-gauge railway from Ravenglass on the coast to the Eskdale valley, terminating at Boot. ☎ 01229 717171. www.ravenglass-railway.co.uk. Admission £6.40/£10.80 adult single/unlimited day travel; £3.20/£5.40 children 5–15 yrs single/unlimited; free under 5 yrs; £27.50 family; £1.50 dogs; £3 cycles per journey.

For other train routes, including the West Coast line, see Getting There (p 175).

By Car
A car can be both a blessing and a burden. It's useful to be able to hop in and out of the car as you please, but peak season/public holidays see plenty of tailbacks and traffic jams in the Lakes and on the motorways en route. Look out for hotels with car parks and then swap your car for public transport while you're there.

There are several companies offering car hire throughout the UK, including Avis ☎ 0844 5810147, www.avis.co.uk; Budget ☎ 0844 5443439, www.budget.co.uk; Europcar ☎ 0870 6075000, www.europcar.co.uk; Hertz ☎ 0870 8448844, www.hertz.co.uk; and National ☎ 0870 4004581, www.nationalcar.co.uk.

For competitive prices on car hire, see www.holidayautos.co.uk.

Driving in the Lake District is fine if you have plenty of patience and are an experienced driver. Try to avoid peak season as the roads can become clogged. Also, make sure your car is roadworthy and able to cope with hairpin bends and steep climbs. Check the oil and fuel levels and the brakes before you set off.

Breakdown cover: Recommendable car rental companies will provide you with a number to call in case of breakdown.

If you're bringing your own car and want cover before you come, try www.roadsideassistance.co.uk for a multi-company quote.

Some places, such as Hardknott Pass, are remote with no petrol stations.

By Ferry
Ferry and steamer services operate on several of the larger lakes.

Coniston Launch (☎ 015394 36216, www.conistonlaunch.co.uk) between Coniston, Waterhead, Torver and Brantwood (p 111).

Keswick Launch (☎ 017687 72263, www.keswick-launch.co.uk) on Derwentwater between Keswick, Nichol End, Hawes End, Low Brandlehow, High Brandlehow, Lodore and Ashness (p 131, **8**).

Steam Yacht Gondola (☎ 015394 41288, www.nationaltrust.org.uk/gondola) between Coniston, Brantwood and Monk Coniston (p 111, **4**).

Ullswater Steamers (☎ 017684 82229, www.ullswater-steamers.co.uk) from Pooley Bridge to Glenridding (p 19).

Windermere Lake Cruises (☎ 015394 43360, www.windermere-lakecruises.co.uk) between Ambleside, Bowness and Lakeside, along with Brockhole and Ferry House (p 12, **1**).

By Bicycle
See 'The Great Outdoors' (p 154).

By Taxi
Below are a few taxi numbers. Alternatively, ask your hotel to call you one.
A2B Taxis (Whitehaven) ☎ 01946 599407
Ambleside Taxis ☎ 015394 33842
Blue Star Taxis ☎ 01539 723670
Bowness Taxis ☎ 015394 46664

Cockermouth Taxi Company
☎ 01900 826649
Davies Taxis (Keswick) ☎ 017687 72676
Derwent Taxis (Keswick) ☎ 017687 75585
Eden Taxis ☎ 01768 865432
Grasmere Taxi Services
☎ 015394 35506
Lake Taxis (Windermere)
☎ 015394 46777
Ulverston Cars ☎ 01229 584565

Fast **Facts**

ATMS   ATMs can be found in main towns, villages, petrol stations and at some shops and hotels throughout the Lake District.

BANKING HOURS   Banks are normally open from 9.30am–1.30pm Mon–Fri although there is some variation.

BIKE RENTALS   See p 157.

BUSINESS HOURS   Shops are usually open 9am–5pm Mon–Sat and from 10am–3pm Sun. In tourist areas shops may remain open later.

CREDIT CARDS   Visa and Master Card are widely accepted in most outlets, and American Express, Diners Club and EuroCard are also accepted at major establishments.

CUSTOMS   If you are travelling outside of the EU, the duty free allowance for adults is 200 cigarettes or 100 cigarillos or 50 cigars or 250g of tobacco, one litre of spirits, one litre of wine with 60ml of perfume and 250ml of eau de toilette.

DOCTOR   See hospitals, below.

ELECTRICITY   240 volts, 50Hz. 13-amp, three-pin, rectangular plugs are used and adapters are easy to find.

EMBASSIES   Full details of all the embassies in the UK can be found on the Foreign and Commonwealth Office website www.fco.gov.uk.

Australia, Australian High Commission, Australia House, Strand, London WC2B 4LA. ☎ 020 7379 4334.

Canada, Canadian High Commission, MacDonald House, 1 Grosvenor Square, London W1K 4AB, ☎ 020 7258 6600.

USA, 24 Grosvenor Square, London W1A 1AE ☎ 020 7499 9000.

EMERGENCY ASSISTANCE   Police, Ambulance, Fire or other Emergency ☎ 999.

GAY & LESBIAN TRAVELLERS   **Homosexuality** is legal in the UK, with the legal age of consent for both men and women being 16. For more information, see www.stonewall. org.uk, www.queery.org.uk and www.tht.org.uk. Or call the Cumbria & Lancashire Lesbian Network on ☎ 01524 858206.

HOSPITALS   see www.nhs.uk for hospitals and doctors (GPs).

Cumberland Infirmary Newtown Road, Carlisle ☎ 01228 523444.

Furness General Hospital Dalton Lane, Barrow-in-Furness ☎ 01229 870870.

Royal Lancaster Infirmary Ashton Road, Lancaster ☎ 01524 65944.

West Cumberland Hospital Homewood, Hensingham, Whitehaven ☎ 01946 693181.

Westmorland General Hospital Burton Road, Kendal ☎ 01539 732288.

There are also a number of health centres and doctors' surgeries in most towns and villages throughout Cumbria where you can see a doctor. Check with your hotel reception, tourist information or telephone directory for details of one closest to where you are staying. Alternatively, see www.nhs.uk, where you can search for hospitals, doctors, dentists and other medical practitioners. Or call NHS Direct on ☎ 0845 4647 for health advice and information.

INSURANCE   Always travel with adequate insurance cover. If you plan to undertake high-risk activities such as climbing or watersports, make sure your policy covers these activities. EU citizens should travel with a European Health Insurance Card (EHIC) which entitles you to free or reduced state medical treatment if you should need care whilst in the UK.

INTERNET ACCESS/CAFES   Most of the main towns have Internet cafés, but local libraries may provide a free service. Many hotels have Internet access and WiFi. Ask when you make your booking.

LOST PROPERTY   Report any losses at the local police station and ask for an incident number if you intend to claim on your insurance. Alternatively, call the Cumbria Constabulary's non-emergency number or see their website for the nearest station. ☎ 0845 3300247. www. cumbria.police.uk.

MAIL & POSTAGE   There are post offices in most main towns and many villages. See www.postoffice. co.uk and click on branch finder, where you can search for the nearest office. Or call ☎ 08457 223344. Post offices are generally open from 9am–5.30pm Mon–Fri, 9am–12.30pm Sat. Some bigger post offices have longer opening hours and smaller ones less.

MONEY & EXCHANGE BUREAUX   The UK's currency is the pound sterling. One pound is divided into 100 pennies or pence. Notes in circulation come in £5, £10, £20 and £50 denominations and there are 1p, 2p, 5p, 10p, 20p, 50p, £1 and £2 coins. There are exchange bureaux at all airports. Most major banks will also exchange money for you.

PARKING   In towns, many car parks are operated by the local council and you will need to buy a ticket. On-street parking may be restricted to residents. Always check first — if you are in violation of the regulations then you might find yourself with a parking ticket, which will be much more expensive than the cost of parking.

In the countryside, car parking rates vary depending on who owns or operates them. Some car parks are operated by the Lake District National Park and the National Trust, among others. Charges are at least £1.50 up to 1 hour, £2.20 up to 2 hours, £4 up to 4 hours. Make sure you have a valid ticket and return to your car within the specified time or you could find yourself paying a fine, being clamped or towed away.

PHARMACIES   Pharmacies, or chemists as they are often called, are found throughout the Lake District and are open during normal shopping hours. Boots The Chemists is open on a Sunday from 10am–4pm. Alternatively, ask at your hotel or contact NHS Direct ☎ 0845 4647,

www.nhs.uk/servicedirectories/
Pages/ServiceSearch.aspx.

POLICE   See emergency assistance.

SAFETY   The Lake District has a relatively low crime rate. However, visitors should take the usual precautions with valuables and personal safety.

SENIOR TRAVELLERS   The Lake District is a popular destination for all ages and anyone over 60 is entitled to discounts at many attractions and museums.

SHOPPING   Details on shopping can be found throughout this book, with an emphasis on individual and unique shops.

For farmers' markets, see p 183. There are also general household, food and other markets in various towns from approximately 9am–4.30pm, including:

Ambleside, King Street car park — Wed.

Barrow-in-Furness, Duke Street — Mon, Wed, Fri and Sat.

Kendal, Indoor Market — Mon–Sat.

Keswick, Main Street (around Moot Hall) — Sat.

Ulverston, Market Street and New Market Street — Wed and Sat.

Whitehaven, Main Street — Thurs and Sat.

SMOKING   Smoking is not allowed in any bar, restaurant or entertainment establishment unless there is a smoking-designated area.

STAYING HEALTHY   Standards of health and hygiene are high in the UK. However, during the summer months, visitors should take care against the sun, which can be deceptively hot, even when it is overcast. Wear a suitable factor sunscreen when out walking or playing watersports. A sun hat is advisable, and if you are travelling with children, be aware that they, especially babies,

need extra protection. Remember to drink plenty of water to replace lost fluids. You should also come prepared for the rain and cold, especially if you are walking on the fells. It might be warm on lower ground but the temperature can fall rapidly on higher ground. If you have any concerns, call NHS Direct.

TELEPHONES   Public phones are located all around the Lake District, and you'll still see a few of the old red telephone boxes.

TIME   The UK is on Greenwich Mean Time (GMT) in winter and British Summer Time (one hour ahead) between the last Sunday in March and the last Sunday in October. The UK is five hours ahead of Eastern Standard Time in winter. For a time check ☎ 123.

TIPPING   As with the rest of the UK, gratuities in the Lake District should be in the region of 10%.

TRAVELLERS WITH DISABILITIES   If you have a disability or any specific needs, contact Disability Information — a UK-based organization dedicated to disabled persons in the United Kingdom — before you travel. ☎ 01332 295551, minicom ☎ 01332 295581, www.disability information.com. If you require any assistance at the airport, notify your airline before you fly as they will inform the airport directly.

USEFUL PHONE NUMBERS   **Directory Enquires** There are several services, all with individual charges. The cheapest is ☎ 118 226 followed by ☎ 118 390, ☎ 118 848, ☎ 118 500 and ☎ 118 118, in order of cost. Or look online for free www.bt.com. Or www.yell.com for business numbers.

VAT   The current rate of VAT is 15%, although this is due to return to the previous rate of 17.5% in

2010. Food (except in restaurants or takeaways), books and newspapers, children's clothes and shoes and public transport are all zero rated.

WATER   Tap water is generally safe to drink. There is a wide range of local and imported still and sparkling bottled waters available throughout the Lake District. Large supermarkets are generally cheaper.

Lake District: **A Brief History**

6000 BC–3000 BC Neolithic settlements emerge around Cockermouth, Keswick, Penrith, Sellerfield, Shap and Ulverston, leaving behind stone circles, axe heads and other remains.

1ST CENTURY The Celtic tribe, Brigantes, rule most of Northern England, including Cumbria.

1ST–2ND CENTURIES Romans build forts at Ambleside, Hardknott, Ravenglass and other locations as part of the Hadrian's Wall defences.

5TH–8TH CENTURY The Celtic Kingdom of Rheged dominates north-west England.

7TH CENTURY Angles come to Eden Valley from north-east England, St Oswald (King of Northumbria) preaches at Grasmere, and Saint Cuthbert granted lands in Cartmel.

10TH CENTURY Viking settlers reach Cumbria; Herdwick sheep introduced to region.

11TH CENTURY Normans gain control over Cumbria.

11TH–17TH CENTURIES Conflict between England and Scotland persists over ownership of Northern England.

12TH CENTURY Cartmel Priory, Furness Abbey and Shap Abbey founded. First slate mines in Honister and coal in Whitehaven.

15TH–16TH CENTURIES Fortified 'pele' towers are built as a

Cumbrian Dialect

Cumbria's dialect developed over centuries of influence by its neighbours, residents and settlers. In the 5th century, the people of the Kingdom of Rheged spoke a dialect of the Celtic language Brythonic (which became Old Welsh), but by the 10th century, Old Norse was more dominant, followed by English, which became the main language. Celtic and Norse influences still exist, although the hilly terrain means there are variations in both dialect and accent. This is particularly obvious in the varied system of counting — of sheep, in games, knitting and fishing, among other things. In Keswick, one to five is 'yan, tyan, tethera, methera, pimp', but in Wasdale, 'yan, taen, tudder, anudder, nimph'. To learn more, see www.lakelanddialectsociety.co.uk

defence against the Scots. Graphite mined in Borrowdale, leading to the pencil industry.

1536–37 Cartmel Priory is surrendered during the Dissolution of the Monasteries.

1650 George Fox, the 'founder' of the Quakers, preaches at Pardshaw Crag.

1806 Building begins on the present Lowther Castle, near Penrith.

1835 William Wordsworth's *Guide to the Lakes* is published, attracting visitors to the region.

1846–7 Kendal and Windermere rail links open.

1850 William Wordsworth dies.

1895 National Trust is founded.

1900 John Ruskin dies.

1930–47 Arthur Ransome publishes his *Swallows and Amazons* books.

1943 Beatrix Potter dies, leaving large areas of land to the National Trust.

1951 Lake District National Park established.

1952 & 1965 Alfred Wainwright's *Pictorial Guide to the Lakes* is published.

1967 Donald Campbell dies while trying to break the world water-speed record on Coniston Water.

1970 Lancaster–Penrith section of the M6 motorway completed.

1974 Cumbria formed from the former counties of Cumberland, Westmorland and parts of North Lancashire and North Yorkshire.

1979 Long Meg Mine closes at Little Salkeld.

1983 Cumbria's last deep coal mine, the Haig Pit at Whitehaven, closes.

2001 Foot and mouth disease leads to thousands of animals being destroyed, and also has a devastating effect on the tourism industry.

2001 Donald Campbell's body recovered from Coniston Water; he is buried later that year in Coniston cemetery.

Lake District **Cuisine**

The Lake District lies at the heart of Cumbria, which came into existence as a county in 1974 when the counties of Cumberland, Westmorland and parts of Lancashire and Yorkshire were merged. So, in the Lakes you'll find a combination of specialties from these different areas. Follow our foodies trail (p 48) to taste some of these, including locally produced chutneys to ice cream and beer.

Breads & Sweets
Apple tansy — dessert made from apples, breadcrumbs, cream, sugar, lemon and nutmeg.
Cumberland Rum Nicky — pastry filled with dates, ginger and rum.

Cumbrian oatcakes — similar to Scottish oatcakes and served with cheese.
Damson cobbler — sweet scones cooked in pureed damsons (often known here as Witherslacks).

Gingerbread — from the famous Grasmere Gingerbread shop (p 115, ④).

Kendal Mint Cake — mint-flavoured sugary candy, sometimes covered in chocolate, and often taken to provide energy on the fells.

Preserves, jams, jellies and 'cheeses' — look out for fruit jam, marmalade, jelly and cheese or curd (smoother, more like a puree and served with bread).

Breweries

Barngates Brewery — Crackers, Chesters, Tag Lag, Cat Nap, Westmorland Gold, Red Bull Terrier, K9, 1077. www.barngatesbrewery.co.uk.

Coniston Brewing Company — Bluebird Bitter, Blacksmith Ale, Old Man Ale, Special Oatmeal Stout, Oliver's Light Ale, Winter Warmer Blacksmith's Ale. www.coniston brewery.co.uk (p 51).

Hesket Newmarket Brewery — Blencathra Bitter, Catbells Pale Ale, Great Cockup Porter, Old Carrock Strong Ale, Scafell Blonde, Helvellyn Gold, Skiddaw, Haystacks. www. hesketbrewery.co.uk.

Jennings Brewery — Cumberland, Sneck Lifter, Cocker Hooper, Bitter and seasonal ales. www.jennings brewery.co.uk (p 50).

Keswick Brewing Company — seasonal and changing Thirst beers. www.keswickbrewery.co.uk.

Kirkstile Inn — Melbreak Bitter, Grasmoor Dark Ale, Rannerdale, Kirkstile. www.kirkstile.com.

Dairy

Abbott Lodge Jersey Ice Cream — at the ice cream farm (p 60). www. abbottlodgejerseyicecream.co.uk

Cheeses — cow's cheese such as Cumberland farmhouse and Lake District extra mature, Allerdale goats cheese, Blengdale blue cheese.

Windermere Ice Cream — all over the Lake District, based at Staveley (p 53). www.scoopchoice.co.uk

Farmers' Markets

Cockermouth — 1st Saturday of the month 9.30am–2pm.

Egremont — 1st and 3rd Friday of the month.

Kendal — 2nd Friday of the month.

Penrith — 3rd Tuesday of the month 9.30am–2pm.

Pooley Bridge — Last Sunday of the month Apr–Sep 10.30am–2.30pm.

Ulverston Food Fair — 2nd Saturday of the month (from Mar) 10am–3pm.

Farms & Shops

Cranston's Ullswater Road, Penrith. ☎ 01768 868680. www. cranstons.net. Open Mon–Sat 8am–6pm.

Greystone House Farm Shop & Tearoom Greystone. ☎ 01768 866952. www.greystonehousefarm. co.uk. Open daily 10am–5.30pm.

Hawkshead Relish The Square, Hawkshead. ☎ 015394 36614. www.hawksheadrelish.com.

Holker Food Hall Holker Estate, Cark-in-Cartmel, Nr Grange-over-Sands. ☎ 015395 58378. www. holker.co.uk.

Low Sizergh Barn Low Sizergh Farm, Sizergh, Kendal. ☎ 015395 60426. www.lowsizerghbarn.co.uk. Open daily 9am–5pm. (until 5.30pm Easter–Dec).

Plumgarths Farm Shop Lakelands Food Park, Kendal. ☎ 01539 736300. Open Mon–Sat 9am–5pm. www. plumgarths.co.uk.

Rheged Redhills, Penrith. ☎ 01768 868000. www.rheged.com.

Sillfield Farm Endmoor, Kendal. ☎ 015395 67609. Open Fri–Sat 10am–5pm; Sun 10am–4pm. www. sillfield.co.uk.

Staveley Mill Yard Staveley. ☎ 01539 821234. www.staveley millyard.com.

The Village Bakery Melmerby. ☎ 01768 898437. www.village-bakery.com. Open Mon–Sat 8.30am–5pm; Sun 9.30am–5pm.

Yew Tree Farm Heritage Meats
Coniston ☎ 015394 41433. www.
heritagemeats.co.uk.

Meat, Fish & Savouries

Beef and wild game — butchers
shops make them into pies but look
out for restaurants serving their
own recipe stews, roasts and pan-
fried game with rich sauces.

Chutneys and pickles — made with
apple, ginger, other fruit and spices
all over the region.

Cumberland mustard — there is an
age-old recipe for this grainy mustard; the perfect accompaniment to
the Cumberland sausage.

Cumberland sausage — pork
sausage meat with spices made in a
spiral and often cooked whole.
Some are so large that just one
could feed a family.

Herdwick lamb — from the hardy
Herdwick breed of sheep. www.
herdwick-sheep.co.uk.

Salmon and shrimp — from the
lakes and Irish Sea.

Trout — from the lakes, particularly
Esthwaite Water.

**Westmorland mutton and potato
pie** — layers of lamb or mutton with
black pudding, pickled cabbage,
sliced potatoes and onions.

Index

A

Abbott Hall Art Gallery (Kendal), 26, 71, 124–126

Abbott Lodge Jersey Ice Cream, 5, 53, 183

Accommodations, 9–10. *See also* B&Bs
Ambleside, 99–101
Bowness-on-Windermere, 104–105
catering to children, 9–10
in Central Lake District, 68–69
Cockermouth, 108–109
Coniston, 112–113
East Lakes, 76–77
Grasmere, 116–117
Hawkshead, 120–121
Kendal, 126–127
Keswick, 132–133
North Lake, 82–83
Penrith, 136–137
private rentals, 83
South Lake, 94
Ulverston, 142–143
Western Lakes & Cumbrian Coast, 88–89
Whitehaven, 146

Acland, Cubby, 99

Adventure sports, 162–163

Aira Force (Ullswater), 75, 150

Airports, 174

Air travel, 174–175

Allan Bank, 131

Ambleside, 13, 18–19, 24, 63–64

Ambleside Roman Fort, 13, 64, 98, 99

Animal parks. *See* Zoos and animal parks

Aquariums, 12, 56, 65, 85

Architecture
Blackwell (Bowness-on-Windermere), 24, 45–46
Sizergh Castle, 91

Argyle Street (birthplace of Stan Laurel) (Ulverston), 141–142

Armitt, Louisa, 97

Armitt Museum (Ambleside), 13, 97

Art galleries and museums

Abbott Hall Art Gallery (Kendal), 26, 71, 125–126

Armitt Museum (Ambleside), 13, 97

Beacon Museum (Whitehaven), 27, 58, 85, 145

Beatrix Potter Gallery (Hawkshead), 15, 32, 66, 120

Grasmere Village Hall, 117

Heaton Cooper Studio (Grasmere), 116

Keswick Museum & Art Gallery, 13, 80, 129

Moot Hall (Keswick), 129

Ruskin Museum (Coniston), 24, 66, 110–111

William Wordsworth Museum & Art Gallery (Grasmere), 18, 39, 63, 114

Askham, 73

Askham Fell, 73

ATMs, 178

Augustus, George, 43

Automobile museums, 13, 80, 93, 130

B

Bacon, Francis, 41

Banking, 178

Barnsgates Brewery, 183

Bars. *See* Pubs and breweries

Bassenthwaite Lake, 79

B&Bs

Anne Tyson's House (Hawkshead), 120

Armidale Cottages (Maryport), 88

Bay Horse (Ravenglass), 88

Beech House (Kendal), 126

Beech Tree House (Coniston), 112

Blenheim Lodge (Bowness-on-Windermere), 104

Blue Swallow Guest House (Penrith), 136

Bramblewood Cottage Guest House (Keswick), 132

Caledonia Guest House (Penrith), 136

Crown Inn Hotel (Coniston), 113

Deepdale Hall (Ullswater), 76

Eagle & Child Inn (Staveley), 76

Glenfield Guest House (Back Corkickle), 146

Greystone Cottage (Windermere), 105

Hill Crest Country Guest House (Newby Bridge), 94

Hillside Bed & Breakfast (Kendal), 127

Honeysuckle Barn (Ulverston), 142

Howe Keld (Keswick), 132

Lowthwaite B and B (Ullswater), 76–77

Old Vicarage (Lorton), 82

Orchard House (Ulverston), 142

Randy Pike, 117

Rose Cottage (Cockermouth), 109

Stanley House (Eskdale), 89

Town House (Ulverston), 143

Wateredge Inn (Ambleside), 101

Woolpack Inn (Hardknott), 89

Yewfield Vegetarian (Hawkshead), 69

Yew Tree Farm (Coniston), 113

Beaches, 165

Beacon Bakery, 136

Beacon Museum (Whitehaven), 27, 58, 60, 85, 145

Beatrix Potter Gallery (Hawkshead), 15, 32, 66, 120

Bicycle rental and repairs, 130, 157, 178

Bicycling, 10, 65, 67, 80, 81, 86, 154–157, 178

Bird of Prey Centre (Lowther), 60

Birdwatching, 159

Bitter End pub (Cockermouth), 108

Black Bull Inn & Hotel (Coniston), 6, 51, 66, 113

Blackhall Yard (Kendal), 125

Photo **Credits**

Notes

Notes

day BY day™

Get the best of a city or region in 1, 2 or 3 days

Day by Day Destinations include:

Europe
Amsterdam
Athens
Barcelona
Berlin
Brussels & Bruges
Budapest
Cornwall
Dublin
Edinburgh & Glasgow
Florence & Tuscany
Lake District
Lisbon
London
Madrid
Malta & Gozo
Moscow
Paris
St Petersburg

Prague
Provence & the Riviera
Rome
Seville
Stockholm
Valencia
Venice
Vienna

Canada and The Americas

Boston
Cancun &
the Yucatan
Chicago
Honolulu & Oahu
Los Angeles
Las Vegas
Maui

Montreal
Napa & Sonoma
New York City
San Diego
San Francisco
Seattle
Washington

Rest of the World

Bangkok
Beijing
Hong Kong
Melbourne
Shanghai
Sydney
Toronto

Frommer's®

Available wherever books are sold

Explore over 3,500 destinations.

Frommers.com makes it easy.

Find a destination. ✓ Book a trip. ✓ Get hot travel deals.
Buy a guidebook. ✓ Enter to win vacations. ✓ Listen to podcasts.
Check out the latest travel news. ✓ Share trip photos and memories.
And much more.

Frommers.com